THESE ARE THE BREAKS!

A Memoir of Resilience, Passion, and Power

Lino "Lean Rock" Delgado & Paul Vincent Ruma

Text

Lino Delgado & Paul Vincent Ruma

Graphic Design

Sebastián Esguerra

Typeset

Owners - Designed by Jeremy Mickel. From MCKL
Scala - Designed by Martin Majoor. From Martin Majoor

Copy editing

Jeanette Desser

Cover & Mix Photos

Sebastián Esguerra for BREAKERS Collective
Paris, FR (2024)

Editorial Operations

El-Houari Si Abdelkader

ISBN

978-1-967635-01-6

TABLE OF CONTENTS

ACKNOWLEDGMENTS

I want to express my deepest gratitude to all those who supported me throughout the writing of this memoir. The journey was no easy feat, and I extend my heartfelt thanks to everyone who uplifted me, making the process rewarding. Your encouragement served as the backbone of this memoir.

To my incredible parents, Ivy and Lino, thank you for the support since birth. I genuinely appreciate your efforts in guiding me along a path I'm proud to tread. Growing older, I'm very thankful for your love, the environment you provided, and for being the best parents anyone could ask for. To my grandparents, aunts, uncles, cousins, godparents, and sister Madelyn, your teachings on unconditional love fill my life with a profound sense of love. The insights shared during the interviews I conducted with most of you ensured that this memoir reflects the truth as accurately as possible.

I am grateful to my friends Deby Barnes, Raymond Cham, RoxRite, Kid David, Shiva, Nadir, Olivia Dominguez, Dom Dorais, Bryan Davila, Celskiii, Oriana FeenX, Lauryn Speights, MG, Wary, and Junior Rock. Your assistance added value to this memoir, creating a space for me to learn and grow. I'm forever grateful for the time and effort you dedicated to helping me in this process, showering it with light and love.

Special thanks to the professionals who offered their insights: Donielle Prince, Storm, Ken Swift, Dart Adams, House Magana, Joe Schloss, Rhettmatic, Akrobatik, Delrokz, Emery Petchauer, Imani Kai Johnson, and Mary Fogarty. Your contributions to my memoir have been game-changers in shaping this book. I extend my gratitude to you all for recognizing the significance of education in Hip Hop culture, mental health, and the importance of overcoming struggles.

I also appreciate the vital roles played by our copy editor, Jeanette Desser, and contributors such as B-boy Abide, Paress Salinas, Bohnna Chhim, Bryan Davila, Pauline Ellis, Moshe Amundson, Deby Barnes, Nora Diggelman, Linda Sharp, Ryan Woodcock, Atiya Niles, Min Kim, Jason Schneider, Jonathan Farwell, Peter Perrault, Jonathan Christian, London Reyes, Jay Taj, Alex Diaz, Paul Russavage, Navid Najafi, Peter Kang, Dash Montalvo, Boaz Rosen, Erica Mack, Candy Foelix, Greg Selkoe, LeeJ Razalan Jr., Mekella Peach, Philip "Spee-d" Albuquerque, Ronnie Abaldonado, Bruno Ribeiro, and Mitchel Dumlao for their generous contributions, making this memoir a reality.

Lastly, thank you to all the readers who will embark on this journey with me. Writing this memoir has been a life-changing experience, and I'm honored to share it with each of you.

FOREWORD

by Ken Swift

We've all heard many b-boys and b-girls say, "Hip Hop saved my life"; some use the term loosely, but there are many that mean it fully. Hip Hop can be your superpower, your therapy, your escape, your spirituality, and your highest high. But sometimes, Hip Hop can disrupt your life, create problems in relationships, cause confrontations or jealousy, and enable unhealthy lifestyles. Hip Hop can take you on a journey, but the art can bring you back to your best self over and over again.

Mental health is a topic that we all experience but won't talk about at a jam or party. Hip Hop was founded partly as an outlet and protest to the trauma and abuse of the streets of NYC in the 1970s. We were all damaged by life and circumstance but shared a love of the arts that kept us striving for something different, even though we didn't really know what this would all become. Some of the pioneers of this culture succumbed to the worst of street culture and either passed away too young, ended up in long stints in prison, or long struggles with addiction.

Even the trauma of losing so many brothers and sisters, to this day, has challenged my mental health and sobriety. But the fight is always in me; the battle is ongoing, and I refuse to lose. By acknowledging the roots of our trauma and seeing how far we've come, we can deal with issues with positive choices and win the battle again and again.

This book is Lean Rock's story. Over the years, I've watched his growth as an artist, as a person, and as a professional. He is a talented b-boy and equally talented as a DJ at a high level. He has always been a dedicated student of Hip Hop and has elevated his skills to be recognized and celebrated worldwide.

Hip Hop history is a difficult puzzle to piece together, as it is mostly passed through word of mouth and a current lived experience; sometimes, this is honest and truthful, and other times inflated and full of lies. We have also lost so many powerful and prolific artists who helped build this culture, and with them, we lost so much of their story and personal histories. Lean's attempt to document his experience is as close as we can really get to the history of these art forms. It is first about people and perspective, and then it is about our collective on a community and global scale.

But as people, we live, we work, we struggle, we have pain, we fall, we grow, we heal, we get back up. Regardless of our individual journey, the story of Hip Hop is a story of overcoming obstacles, making something out of nothing, carving your own path, and surviving trauma to create something better.

This is not only a reflection of the journey he's still on but also a story of his father's experiences as a pioneering Hip Hop artist. It covers raising his son, their shared love of breaking and DJing, the underground business of Hip Hop events and music, and the history of Boston's Hip Hop community. There is a detailed history of lineage and contributions of the Floor Lords and their consistent integrity over decades of being a true influential crew in the community and the world. Part memoir storytelling and personal ancestry, part history from his perspective on breaking from the time he was four years old, part historical documentation through appreciation to his mentors and influences, part educational text and skill-building for practitioners, this book is also a self-help motivational story of mental health struggles and survival through finding techniques to find his own mental stability and peace. It is Lean Rock's legacy, his thesis, his reflection on his life, and his manifesto.

Hip Hop culture is about utilizing the arts and culture of Hip Hop to create peace, love, unity, and having fun. This book is Lean Rock's gift to our community—calling attention to mental health, which is prominent in Hip Hop and beyond, and sharing his own vulnerability to have us all see ourselves in his resilience. If it helps anyone in their own journey to mental health and well-being, then it has done its job, and the ripple effects can change lives to make us a stronger community.

Ken Swift VII Gems, NYC

A BREAKING POINT

An hour after taking an edible, my vision blurred, and distant dog barks echoed in my ears. I imagined a SWAT team outside, ready to bust in. As paranoia overwhelmed me, my blood pressure spiked, feeling as if I were about to have a heart attack. I felt like I had done something terribly wrong, and I kept thinking, "This is it, I'm going to die." I suspected my girlfriend had set me up. As she sat on top of me, I looked directly into her eyes, thinking I saw a demon.

Terrified, I cried out for help, yelling, "Stop! Please stop!" My paranoia intensified whenever I tried to snap out of the high, and my heart raced. I begged God, "Please bring me back to normality!" Not knowing I was experiencing an anxiety attack since I had never had one before, I later discovered I had also suffered a psychotic episode. After hours of mental struggle, I forced myself to sleep.

Following that experience, I decided to go sober. However, even that wasn't enough, as I remained paranoid, looking around everywhere, thinking the government and people were trying to kill me. Watching TV or witnessing any activities happening in the streets would trigger me. It felt as if an evil spirit followed me everywhere I went, like hell on earth. A week and a half later, the situation reached its breaking point while I was heading to the airport for my annual summer European tour.

Suddenly, I experienced another anxiety attack and psychotic episode. I began crying hysterically. Despite having gone sober, I believed my mind was gone forever and that people were still after me. The only way I could describe this feeling was like when you're a kid watching a scary movie, covering your eyes and praying for the gruesome scene to end. My girlfriend rushed me to Cedars-Sinai Medical Center, running red lights and breaking the speed limit. As soon as I arrived, I pleaded with the doctors, "Please God help me! Stop this from happening! I can't live like this anymore!"

CHAPTER 1

LINEAGE

Going sober was the first step. But even that wasn't enough. The paranoia lingered. The fear. The feeling that I had lost something in myself that I might never get back. My entire life, I had been moving at full speed, touring the world, DJing at events, chasing the next gig, the next city, the next moment. And now, for the first time, I was forced to slow down. The silence was unbearable.

I had spent years defining myself through music, through movement, through the energy of a crowd. But who was I when the music stopped? When the lights were off and I was alone? I had spent my entire life mastering my craft, but I had never mastered how to just be.

In that stillness, I had to face a truth I had been avoiding for years. Everything I had built, everything I had become, was shaped by what came before me. If I wanted to understand how I got here, how I reached this breaking point, I had to go back to the very beginning. I had to go back to my family.

As I traced my steps back, I realized that the answers I was seeking were tied to the history of my family. Understanding the root causes of our mental health challenges is crucial to making logical and informed decisions. In my family, a legacy of abuse, abandonment, mental health problems, addiction, and post-traumatic stress disorder has persisted across generations. Writing this book helped me realize the importance of identifying and breaking the cycle of trauma.

Sometimes, we unintentionally continue the pain that our family experienced by repeating the same harmful behaviors in our own lives. I found it necessary to investigate my family history and pay attention to recurring life patterns to gain clarity about myself. By asking my relatives about our past, I could piece together parts of my "life puzzle" and better comprehend my own anxiety. As I always say, the answers to our struggles can be found in the past.

• My grandparents, Orfelina Delgado and Lino Delgado Sr., dancing together in Boston, MA (late 1990s).

My Father's Side

I proudly trace my heritage back to my Afro-Latino grandmother, Orfelina, who was born in Santo Domingo, Dominican Republic, and my grandfather, Lino, in the countryside of Caguas, Puerto Rico. They both migrated to New York City, where on January 27, 1967, my dad, Lino Delgado Jr, was born in Brentwood, Long Island. He was the fourth child in a family of five siblings born in the 1960s. Unfortunately, my family faced financial hardships during this time. My grandfather also struggled with alcoholism and was absent for a significant portion of my father's childhood. As a result, my dad always aimed to be the father his own dad could not be.

In 1973, my grandmother's life took a turn for the worse when she entered a relationship with an abusive man. With no plan and nowhere to live, he uprooted the family, forcing them to move into her cousin's family home in Boston. They had to leave most of their belongings outside until they could find a place of their own. During this time, neighbors attempted to steal their furniture, so my family had to guard it for an entire month.

After my family relocated from New York to Boston, they experienced intense racism, particularly during the Boston desegregation busing crisis. Living in a neighborhood that was predominantly white on one side and Black on the other, my dad's family, one of the few Latino families in the area, endured physical threats and racial slurs. I've heard painful stories about how my dad and his siblings had to fist-fight with people while getting on and off the school bus, as well as during school hours. It was a life or death situation just to complete a simple task. Despite being known as a liberal city, the Boston desegregation busing crisis of the 1970s and 1980s deeply impacted many people of color through physical violence, emotional trauma, and educational disruption. These stories of struggle were more than just history lessons for me. They were part of my family's lived experience, shaping the way I understood race and identity from an early age.

As I grew up, that understanding deepened when I joined the Club48 after-school program, which provided historical education on racism and its ongoing effects on society. It was a predominantly Black program that took us on trips to places like the Harriet Tubman House in the South End of Boston. Walking through its museum-like exhibits, surrounded by photographs, artifacts, and firsthand accounts of struggle, I gained a deeper awareness of the systemic racism that had shaped generations before me, including my own family's experiences. Though I was only seven years old, I couldn't help but think about the stories I had heard from my father. He and his siblings had to fight just to get on and off the school bus, and my grandmother had endured her own battles at home.

Long before I was born, my family was already navigating a world determined to break them. While my dad and his siblings fought for their place in a deeply segregated city, my grandmother was battling something entirely different behind closed doors. For years, she suffered physical abuse at the hands of my dad's "stepfather" before finally finding the strength to leave him. The violence my family faced wasn't just external; it was inescapable, seeping into both their public and private lives. It's hard for me to fully fathom how traumatic that must have been for them.

For a short stint, my grandmother lived in her own home in Dorchester, Massachusetts, before ultimately settling in the South End of Boston in 1979. Nine years later, my grandfather reunited with the family and returned to my dad's life. This reunion was emotional for both my dad and my grandmother. While my grandmother was grateful for his return, my grandfather was still struggling with alcohol addiction at the time. My dad found it difficult to reconnect after so many years apart, but over time, their relationship grew stronger, especially as my grandfather overcame his struggles and embraced sobriety.

• My grandmother, Orfelina, at my kindergarten graduation (1995).

The reunion between my grandparents marked the beginning of a renewed bond, but it was my grandmother Orfelina's unwavering strength, faith, and love that truly shaped our family. She became a major inspiration in my life, raising generations with her kindness and devotion. Everyone who entered her home was embraced and nurtured. Her dedication to God was second to none, as she would pray for my family for hours each day. My grandmother was the epitome of unconditional love.

She would cook breakfast, lunch, and dinner for the entire family every day. No one ever left her house hungry. She cooked the best meals with all of her heart. Later in life, I followed in her footsteps. Whether cooking for others or taking them to the best restaurant in town, I learned that food is essential to people's hearts and happiness. She was my mentor in unconditional love.

• My grandmother Stephanie Henn in Las Vegas, NV (1967).

My Mother's Side

Just as my grandmother Orfelina shaped my values through her love and devotion, my maternal grandmother, Stephanie Henn, carried her own profound experiences that shaped our family's history. While Orfelina nurtured with faith and food, Stephanie's journey was one of resilience in the face of hardship. Her story, though different, is just as integral to the foundation of who I am today.

My grandmother, Stephanie Henn, was born in Orange, New Jersey, in 1945 to parents of British, Irish, German, and French ancestry. Her childhood was normal until her father, Robert Henn, died in a freak boating accident on her tenth birthday, causing her to suffer from depression. My great-grandfather and grandmother had a strong bond, and she was devastated by his death. The impact of his absence on my family is something that I often ponder, and my grandmother's admiration for him suggests that he was a loving man who cherished his family. Unfortunately, things got worse for my grandmother when she was subjected to physical and emotional abuse by her stepfather until she graduated from high school.

Following her graduation, she decided to travel around the country to soul search and spent a few years in Honolulu, Hawai'i, in the mid-1960s before ultimately settling in San Francisco by the late 1960s. During her time there, my grandmother met my grandfather, Sang Lee. My grandmother gave birth to my mother, Ivy Lee, and aunt, Heather Lee, in January 1972. Two years later, she left San Francisco and moved to Boston to raise her daughters on her own. We never had any contact with my grandfather or his side of the family.

Due to my grandmother's deep depression and mental instability, she was unable to care for my mom and aunt. As a result, a family by the name of Miller from Needham, Massachusetts, adopted them as toddlers, while my grandmother dealt with her issues. Despite this, my mom and aunt yearned for their mother, crying daily at the front door and begging for her return until years later when my grandmother was in a better place mentally and able to reunite with her family. They moved to the South End, but shortly after, my grandmother's health began to deteriorate due to heart complications and depression once again.

At just eight years old, my mom was forced to take on the household duties, while my grandmother's health continued to decline. With their family struggling financially, my mom had to care for herself and her family, until my grandmother found a new boyfriend during my mother's teenage years in the mid-1980s, who helped to ease the load. Nevertheless, my grandmother's health continued to worsen, and she spent her final years in a wheelchair. Even through her struggles, she always treated her grandchildren with love and care.

These hardships and sacrifices became part of who my mom was. She didn't just inherit strength; she was forged by it. My parents didn't become who they are overnight. The values they carry were shaped by the generations before them. My mom grew up learning resilience the hard way, taking on responsibilities way beyond her years, while my dad's path was all about movement, music, and a love for Hip Hop. If my mom's strength came from the sacrifices she made for her family, my dad's resilience was built through the beats and battles that defined his world. In their own ways, they were both shaped by the ones who came before them.

• My dad Lino Delgado Jr. dancing in downtown Boston (1982).

My Parents

My dad's passion for dance and music is infectious. No matter where we go, whether it's the grocery store, clothing store, or a restaurant, he's always moving to the music. His devotion to Hip Hop culture runs deep, and he's always blasting music in his car. Watching him in action has shown me what true passion and humility look like. Despite his age, he never slows down.

He has a humbling spirit and instilled in me the value of always striving for improvement. Whenever I achieved a win in basketball or a breaking battle, he would congratulate me, but also remind me to never become overconfident. If he saw me being too cocky, he would shut me down quickly and say, "Stop talking and let the skills do the talking." His blunt honesty always comes from a place of love and his words always resonate with me.

Growing up, my father had to endure a lot of hardship, but he never let it break him. He always managed to put on a brave face and be a pillar of strength. He's a man of the people. Rarely does he put himself in front of anyone. His resilience has been a source of inspiration for me throughout my life.

My dad is one of the most selfless people I know. Whether he's feeding people, taking someone under his wing, or just lending an ear to someone in need, my dad is always putting others first. It's no wonder that so many people in the Hip Hop community see him as a father figure or mentor. After all, he's been sharing his knowledge and passion for the culture for over forty years now.

• My mom, Ivy Lee, at my kindergarten graduation in Boston, MA (1995).

Just like my dad, my mom is a selfless and loving person. She's quick to brag about me to anyone who will listen, and she never misses an opportunity to shower me with love and affection. Despite having a demanding job at Boston Medical Center, where she's worked for over 25 years, my mom always finds time to think about others. Whenever we go shopping, she calls her friends to see if there's anything they need or want. Her strong faith in God, which has been a constant source of strength and guidance throughout her turbulent life, is one of the three things she lives for, along with her relationship with my sister Madelyn and me.

My mom's strict and protective nature can sometimes feel overwhelming, but I understand that it stems from a place of love and a desire to keep me safe. I've never been able to leave the house without checking in with her first, but it's reassuring to know that she's always there for me when I need her. My mom was determined to give me a better life than she had, and she believed that education, a comfortable home, and financial stability were key.

She worked hard to provide these things for me, and I'm grateful for the structure and support she gave me as I grew up. She encouraged me to play basketball and other sports, which not only helped me stay active and healthy but also gave me a sense of purpose and motivation. Thanks to her, I had the tools and opportunities to pursue my dreams and build a better future for myself.

During the mid-1980s, my mother found solace from the family trauma at home by dating my father, who lived in the South End. After being in a relationship for a few years, they welcomed me into the world on December 19, 1988. Initially, we lived in a small apartment on Hammond Street with my grandmother Orfelina. Shortly after, we relocated a block over to the Piano Factory, a historical building on Tremont Street that served as a sanctuary for Boston-based artists. When you walked downstairs from the lobby, there was an art gallery full of beautiful paintings.

On Friday nights, art exhibitions and parties were held in the building, showcasing the works of a few famous painters who resided there. Among them was Paul Goodnight, a renowned African American artist whose work is related to the African diaspora, and whose paintings are filled with deep meaning and symbols from African culture. We were fortunate enough to have some of his paintings hanging on our apartment walls. Growing up in an artistic environment was a true blessing.

Although my parents did a great job raising me, their relationship was not the best. I don't have many fond memories of them together, as they split when I was six. Thankfully, their separation did not bother me at that young age, as I knew there was too much friction between them. When they were dating, they were both young, immature, and argumentative, which made their relationship toxic.

My mom didn't share my dad's passion for Hip Hop and often struggled with his lifestyle, while my dad lived for it. She sought stability, and their differences often led to arguments. These tensions would lead to my dad being out drinking late and taking his anger to the streets of Boston. It was not a healthy environment for us, and it seemed like their relationship was headed for a grim ending if they stayed together. Fortunately, after the breakup, I got the best of both worlds when I was with them separately. I inherited creativity from my dad and structure from my mom, and I appreciate the qualities that each of them brought to my life.

Hearing these stories from my family, I came to realize that strength wasn't just about survival. It was about bearing the weight of past generations and carving out a new path, even when it felt impossible. Growing up between my parents' two worlds shaped me, but so did the city around me. Boston, with its struggles, energy, and resilience, became as much a part of my story as the people I grew up with.

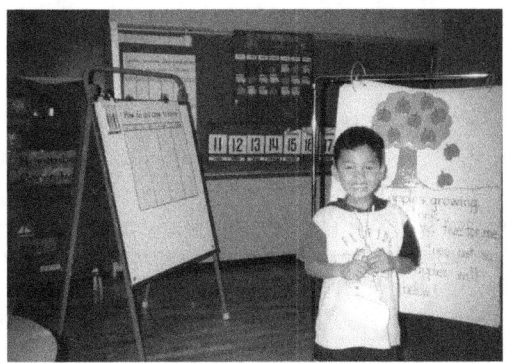

• Me at the Hurley Elementary School in 1st grade (1995).

My Neighborhood

I'm a proud Bostonian, and I want to share my experiences of growing up in the city. To give context, I must go back to what Boston was like around the time I was born. In the late 1980s and early to mid-1990s, the city had its highest crime and murder rates. Gangs and the crack epidemic led to an increase in violence and murders, which didn't mix well with low-income neighborhoods like the South End that lacked opportunities for the youth. Although the Piano Factory provided a safe haven for me, the surrounding neighborhood was plagued by violence and danger.

Right across the street from the Piano Factory was Lenox Street Projects, one of the most dangerous neighborhoods in Boston. It was predominantly a Black neighborhood, where I spent the first nine years of my life. Further east in the South End was the Villa Victoria, a Puerto Rican community that seemed friendly during the day but was also known for its high crime rate, especially at night. In between these two neighborhoods was my elementary school, The Hurley, where all my friends were Black and Puerto Rican.

Although I was just in elementary school, a part of me was drawn to the idea of being a gangster. As kids, we jokingly talked about robbing people, fighting each other, shooting guns, or anything involving violence. We were mimicking the things we heard and saw in our neighborhoods. In that environment, violence and criminal behavior became the norm; it was just another part of daily life. Everyone took pride in knowing how to fight in the hood, and my biggest influence was my dad. He had a reputation as one of the neighborhood's toughest guys, known for his knockout punch.

I admired the respect he earned through his fighting skills. In honor of my dad's reputation in the hood, I got into a few fistfights at school to test my toughness. Interestingly, I never got into much trouble for fighting. The most they did was put me in time-out, send me to the principal, or occasionally call my parents. I was never suspended at The Hurley, which says a lot about how bad Boston's public school system was in the 1990s.

As a child, I would overhear my dad and his friends joking about their fights, but I didn't fully grasp the gravity of the situation. Though my dad earned respect for his fighting skills, he always told me, "While some of these stories may be funny, this life isn't worth praising."

He had his share of close calls, getting shot at and nearly stabbed, all because of fighting. I was too young to experience anything that extreme, but he knew it was only a matter of time before that world could become my reality. He made sure to educate me on the streets, drilling into my head that the gangster life usually leads to jail or death. He never condoned violence and always reminded me, "Be the bigger man unless someone tries to physically harm you."

For my dad, dance was his escape from the gangster world. While he was never fully immersed in that lifestyle, he grew up around it, and many of his fights stemmed from alcohol-fueled frustrations. Like his father before him, alcohol became his weakness. It was a way to numb the pain of losing close friends to murder, jail, and drugs.

After my parents' separation, something changed in him. He started going to church, and at 27, he got completely sober. That decision transformed his life. Thankfully, he used his talents to break free from the cycle of addiction and began providing for our family. With faith guiding him, he helped me avoid the same pitfalls and showed me there was a better way out.

Migration From The City To The Suburbs

My mom and I stayed in Boston for an additional two years, but we eventually had to leave the Piano Factory due to new management taking over and the neighborhood not being the best place to raise a family. Rent had become unaffordable. My mom started dating a new man, who had a house in Stoughton, Massachusetts. In 1997, we moved in with him to provide a life of safety and structure. I continued to attend Hurley Elementary School for another year until I transferred to Gibbons Elementary school in the fourth grade.

For the first time in my life, I felt like I didn't fit in. I was influenced by street culture, while Stoughton is a typical American suburb. Interestingly, the town was named after the first chief justice of the Colonial Courts, William Stoughton, famed for his hardcore stance during the Salem Witch Trials.

Adjusting to life in Stoughton was tough because the kids there were so different from the ones I grew up with. The town was predominantly white, and everything felt unfamiliar. The way they dressed, the way they talked, and even the music they listened to were all different. While I wore the latest Jordans and Ecko and listened to the hottest rap mixtapes, they wore generic brands and had no clue about the tracks I had on repeat. The only thing that bridged the gap between us was sports.

At Gibbons Elementary, in a school with barely any kids of color, I was the only half Puerto Rican, half Dominican student. Most of my classmates didn't even know where Puerto Rico or the Dominican Republic were on a map, so they simply insisted I was Black. Though I was never bullied, subtle racism lingered in Stoughton, especially in how the town's elders treated me and other people of color. Over time, this chipped away at my sense of identity. I felt awkward and out of place because I couldn't connect with the culture around me, which felt almost nonexistent.

Moving to Stoughton also meant seeing my dad less. I spent weekdays with my mom and weekends in Boston with him. Those weekends became my escape. Being back in the city felt like a vacation, a return to the energy and rhythm that made me feel at home. The music, the movement, the culture, it was all a part of me, and I felt a sense of belonging there that I couldn't find in Stoughton. While the quiet of Stoughton often left me feeling disconnected and out of place, it was in Hip Hop that I found a way to express myself and a community where I truly felt at home.

CHAPTER 2

GROWING UP IN HIP HOP CULTURE

• In my b-boy stance at Disney World in Orlando, FL (1995).

From a young age, I was mesmerised by the rhythm of the beats and the artistry of breaking, things that made me feel grounded and alive, no matter where I was. My dad and his friends were always a reminder of that raw energy, and before I knew it, I was hooked.

One of my earliest memories takes me back to when I was four years old. My dad and his friends were blasting Main Source's "Live at the Barbeque" on a boombox, dancing up a storm in our apartment living room in Boston. Their enthusiasm was infectious. My dad's dancing filled the apartment with energy until my mom stormed in, demanding he turn it down, complaining about the noise. These moments, full of authentic expression, fueled my growing passion for Hip Hop, a passion that would continue to shape my life in the years that followed.

This was a familiar scene. My parents often argued over the volume, but I found it hilarious. I'd sit back and giggle, watching the drama unfold. When my dad and his friends eventually left to find a new spot for their party, I seized the opportunity. I popped in one of his old breaking VHS tapes and settled in to watch. Even at that young age, I was captivated.

My childhood playlist was a mix of *Sesame Street, Teenage Mutant Ninja Turtles,* and breaking footage from the legendary Floor Lords. One video in particular stood out. The Floor Lords performed in polka-dot suits to "The Power" by Snap! I was mesmerized by their moves and mimicked every step. No one pushed me to do it. I was drawn to it naturally.

Breaking was the most incredible thing I had ever seen. It was athletic, artistic, and full of energy. It was born in the Bronx in the early 1970s by Black youth and further developed in the late 1970s by Puerto Rican youth, who infused it with elements of salsa and other Latin styles. Their influence helped shape the structured format of breaking we see today: top rock, go-downs, footwork, spins, air moves, and freezes. Most people call it "breakdancing," but this is actually an incorrect term used by the media. The essence of breaking is based on how rhythmically in tune you are with breakbeat music, which is a style of music characterized by the use of short, sampled drum breaks from funk, soul, jazz, rock, and R&B songs. Without timing and rhythm, even the most acrobatic spins and moves in breaking lack depth.

For me, breaking was more than just a dance. My dad and members of the Floor Lords reminded me of superheroes with their incredible physical abilities. I was in awe as I watched them spin and fly through the air, all the while staying perfectly in rhythm with the music. But before the Floor Lords became legends, my dad's journey with street culture had already begun.

In 1978, long before Hip Hop became a widely recognized movement, my dad visited the Bronx and learned how to break from his older cousins in a crew called High Performance. They taught him top rock and footwork, and he immediately fell in love with it. At the time, breaking wasn't known outside of New York, and when he saw another dancer breaking in Boston and getting laughed at, he became too embarrassed to show off his skills in public.

That changed in the early 1980s when breaking took off in Boston. In contrast, the funk style dance called popping was already popular throughout the country, thanks to The Jackson 5's "Dancing Machine" and the TV show *Soul Train.* Kids everywhere were copying the dance moves from *Soul Train.* My dad and his brother Noz were like The Jackson 2, robot-dancing and copying all the moves they saw.

They started as poppers with their crew, the New York Puppeteers, which was all about having fun and impressing girls. They performed at talent shows and family parties, but as more popping crews emerged, my dad and his crew wanted to set themselves apart. So, they began incorporating breaking moves into their performances, which was a unique fusion of the two dance styles. At the time, the early 1980s, there weren't many groups in the Boston area doing this.

When my dad moved to the South End in 1979, he remarked that it felt like a smaller version of New York City due to the influx of New Yorkers who had settled in the neighborhood. In the early 1980s, people could be seen walking around with radios blasting early rap records, breakbeats, and funk. This lively environment inspired my dad and my uncle Noz to learn how to DJ. They were taught by a local and legendary DJ known as Rusty the Toe Jammer.

• The Floor Lords in downtown Boston (1984).

Rusty was known as one of the first local rap acts to record a record and later owned a record store in Roxbury called Funky Fresh Records. They discovered a new passion for DJing and, after months of practice, eventually surpassed most DJs in Boston with their skills. However, my dad's passion for dance began to take precedence over his interest in DJing.

After moving to the South End, he met Cisco and Mad of the Master Break Team. When they suggested making money on the streets, he assumed they meant selling drugs. They laughed and explained they meant street performing. He gave it a shot and was shocked to make nearly $200 a day, a fortune in the 1980s. With that kind of money, they bought new sneakers and outfits daily.

At the same time, the New York Puppeteers were becoming increasingly caught up in the streets. Recognizing that dance could offer a way out, my dad joined forces with the Master Break Team. In 1981, they formed the Floor Lords, intertwining breaking and popping in a unique way that set them apart from other crews. Through their street shows at Faneuil Hall, they quickly gained recognition as some of Boston's best dancers.

Growing up around Hip Hop, shaped by the Floor Lords and my dad, I had my first moment in the spotlight at just four years old. My dad let me do a solo breaking round at the Curley School auditorium in Jamaica Plain while the Floor Lords changed outfits during intermission.

As soon as I stepped on stage, the crowd roared. I felt a rush of excitement and nerves. I spun, stumbled, and tried my best to do a head spin. The energy was unreal. I danced for what felt like three minutes straight before my dad called out, "Come back! Get off the stage!"

I was not ready to leave. The cheers fueled me, and I shook my head, "No!" I had no sense of time. I was just lost in the moment. My dad had to physically yank me off stage, and I cried. The crowd laughed and let out a few "awws." I was banned from performing for two years after this occurred.

In 1995, I finally got my next shot, this time at the annual City Lights Christmas show. City Lights, a nonprofit in the South End, was a space the Floor Lords helped build with Duggan Hill. This time, my dad made sure I was ready. No more rolling on the floor. I had to learn the fundamentals.

After weeks of training with my dad, I stepped on stage alongside my cousins Flight and J-Quest. I followed every move, stuck to the choreography, and held my own. At the end of the show, I was rewarded with a New England Patriots Starter winter coat. At just six years old, I learned my first lesson in entrepreneurship. If you work hard, you get rewarded.

• With my cousins Gio & El Nino in New Jersey (1998).

• With my dad at Ninja B's house (1995).

Training Under My Dad, Leanski

As I immersed myself in Hip Hop, it was inevitable that I would turn to the one person who could help me learn it, my father. He wasn't just my parent, he was my first Hip Hop mentor, and his lessons would become the foundation of my life. He instilled in me the importance of always being a student and constantly expanding my skill set. His philosophy was simple: the more trades you master, the more doors open. He encouraged me to explore different creative paths such as dance, DJing, graphic design, and video editing, pushing me to give everything a try and work hard at it. This mindset not only taught me the value of learning new skills but also showed me how they all connect. Mastering these trades strengthened both my artistry and business, making it easier to create, adapt, and accomplish more on my own.

Beyond skills, he showed me the power of relationships. He was a man of the people, always recognizing others and always giving back. His networking skills have consistently demonstrated that success in networking comes from providing value to others and allowing opportunities to flow from that. I watched him recognize people for their work and contributions to Hip Hop by giving awards at our events since the late 1990s. He has served as a father figure and mentor not only to me but also to many within the Hip Hop community, including legendary breakers such as Kmel, Abstrak, Ivan the Urban Action Figure, and Wicked, among others.

• Saucony Courageous x Floor Lords sneaker collaboration (2006).

His ability to build relationships extended beyond the dance floor. From a young age, he took me to business meetings, showing me firsthand how street smarts and corporate strategy intersect. I vividly remember sitting in on his meetings at the Saucony headquarters when he secured a shoe deal for our crew Floor Lords. I watched him negotiate, ensuring our culture and history were respected. Saucony recognized our impact on Boston's Hip Hop scene since 1981, leading to the creation of the Floor Lords x Courageous sneaker. My dad worked closely with their team, modifying the shoe's weight and comfort for breaking. The limited-edition sneaker, sold exclusively through Zappos.com and Bodega, sold out fast and was later recognized by Complex as one of the 20 Best Saucony Collaborations of All Time. It's even preserved at Harvard's Hip Hop Archive & Research Institute—a testament to his vision and lasting impact.

My dad's vision was built on discipline, especially when it came to the dance. In the late 1990s, my dad set up a practice schedule for the Floor Lords every Tuesday and Thursday from six to nine in the evening, mainly at Hennigan Elementary School. That same practice schedule is still upheld today, no matter the location, with the new generation of the Floor Lords. As a member of the crew, attending practice was a must. Being late or not showing up at all meant losing money from shows or even getting kicked out of the crew.

I remember one time when a crewmate showed up two hours late. My dad checked him for it and made it clear that dance had to be taken seriously. He told him, "You need to be on time like everyone else and take this more seriously. Otherwise, you can't perform with us at shows. I do not want to hear any more excuses!" We all watched from the sidelines, knowing he was not just talking to one person. He was teaching all of us the importance of being punctual.

Practice always followed a structure. We started with thirty minutes of top rock, focusing on timing, groove, and musicality. My dad made sure we weren't just moving but actually dancing, feeling the music like an instrument, playing off its rhythms and wordplay. It was about more than just steps. It was about flow.

After warming up, we moved into solo rounds. Every round had to start with top rock, go-downs, and footwork before anything else. The energy from the top had to carry through the entire set. You couldn't just drill a move in isolation. It had to connect with the music. Every practice felt like a battle or a performance. Full intensity, no half-stepping.

If we were performing, we had to end strong with a freeze directed at the crowd or, in a battle, at an opponent. My dad drilled it into us. Full effort. Full commitment. If a classic breakbeat played in a cipher, I honored my elders by emulating their moves, paying homage to their style. That's something only true students of the dance understand.

The second half of practice focused on crew routines. We had to be sharp, in sync, and ready for anything. Rival crews called us out regularly, and my dad made sure we stayed prepared. That preparation led to countless wins and show bookings. Footwork drills came next. Two, three, four, and six-step rounds in both directions, sometimes fifty rounds deep to the music. Even as kids, we kept up with the adults. Sometimes we pushed through to the point of tears, but those moments made us stronger.

This kind of training sharpened everything: stamina, precision, and control. We weren't just training for battles; we were training to master our freestyle ability. Back then, there weren't many people creating set routines, as making a living off breaking competitions wasn't even an option. You did it for the craft. Freestyling was everything. My dad hated pre-planned sets. He reminded us that we couldn't repeat moves, go-downs, or transitions. Every round needed to bring something fresh and different.

Breaking is like a fight. If you go in with pre-planned punches, you're getting knocked out. Spontaneity makes the dance powerful. But to freestyle, you need a deep vocabulary of movement and a real connection to the music.

Power moves were a steep learning curve: windmills, flares, headspins, halos. At first, I hesitated, afraid of getting hurt, but my dad wouldn't let fear stop me. I'd get frustrated, put my head down, and then get right back to work. What I didn't realize at the time was that learning these moves was just part of the bigger picture. A true b-boy isn't a one-trick pony. You have to train everything, sometimes for hours a day, sometimes for years. Dedication was the only way to reach the next level.

Dedication to training wasn't just about moves and repetition. It was about the flow and the connection to the music. Music was the backbone of our training. My dad curated the music, switching tempos throughout the night. We started slow, warming up to DJ *Cash Money's In Search of Disco Breaks*, then built up the energy with DJ Leacy's high-powered mixes. When it was time for routines, we drilled to 90s Hip Hop and breakbeat mixtapes by DJ Ninja B. Every few weeks, we switched it up to keep the energy fresh. Like a real jam, dead air was never an option.

It was all about being one with the music and expressing yourself in your own unique way. Originality was everything. Biting, or copying another dancer's moves, was a major offense. In my dad's era, people got checked for that, sometimes physically. Even in my time, being called a biter was a serious mark of shame. I remember some b-boys from Self X accusing me of biting. I called out their whole crew on the mic at a jam in Ohio, ready to battle them all. It turned chaotic, but in the end, my stance earned their respect. Years later, I became friends with them. That experience taught me an important lesson. Once you get to know people instead of assuming, you often find common ground.

My dad always pushed us to develop our own style. One method he used was making me break without relying on my head or neck, since I had become too dependent on them. It forced me to think differently and step outside my comfort zone. In Hip Hop, identity is everything. My dad didn't want anyone saying his students copied others. Everyone has their own creative potential; it's just about unlocking it.

Inspiration came from all around. Early breakers drew from Bruce Lee, fighting scenes from Shaw Brothers films, the Nicholas Brothers, the Three Stooges, and beyond. As a kid, I made my X-Men action figures do moves, not by fighting, but by throwing them in the air, making them spin and twist as if they were breaking. I tried to emulate their fluidity and creativity, imagining them pulling off the moves. Creativity in this dance thrives on imagination.

And style? That mattered just as much as the moves. In Hip Hop, looking fresh is part of the culture. I was a sneakerhead. A fresh pair of Jordan 1s through 11s were my go-to. My dad always said the best dancers could throw down without scuffing their sneakers. If I danced with a hat on, I had to keep it on. Every detail mattered. Presentation wasn't just about fashion. It was about showing you cared. The greats like Michael Jackson and James Brown knew this. So did we.

Looking back, I see my dad's tough love for what it was. He pushed me to be the best I could be, even when I couldn't see it myself, because he wanted me to excel and carry on the Floor Lords' tradition with excellence. He still tells me that to this day. Despite his strictness, he also allowed me to explore and grow within my dance. His praise for a dope round was always genuine and motivating. It was this balance in his approach that helped me develop a thicker skin and achieve a world-class level.

My experience of learning breaking was unique because of my close lineage to the origins of the dance. Unlike many who learn about breaking through third hand sources, I was taught from the inside looking in. That gave me a deeper appreciation of the culture and history behind it. This foundation shaped not just my understanding of the dance but also my perspective on its evolution, especially in the 1990s when breaking thrived underground despite its decline in mainstream visibility.

A 1990s Boston B-boy Perspective

Breaking achieved global mainstream popularity in the early 1980s. However, by the late 1980s in the Boston and New York City region, most practitioners had quit breaking and either adapted to normal society or became involved in the negative aspects of street life, such as drugs, gangs, and robberies. This decline was partly due to the perception that breaking was "played out" on the East Coast by 1986, a sentiment that was shared by many in the breaking community. Despite this dark period for breaking, a few individuals, such as my dad, continued to push the dance forward and keep its legacy alive. The impact of this decline on the breaking community was significant, as many talented dancers left the scene and the evolution of the dance was hindered.

After breaking lost its popularity on the East Coast in the late 1980s, my crew, the Floor Lords, had to stay relevant in the changing nightlife scene by incorporating trendy Hip Hop freestyle steps and Housing while still keeping breaking in their performances. During this dark period, the Floor Lords were one of the few groups in New England that kept the spirit of breaking alive through their nightclub shows. Several individuals and crews from this era played a crucial role in shaping both my breaking and the Boston region. The following section pays tribute to these 1990s greats who significantly influenced my journey.

• With Float at my baptism in Boston, MA (1989).

My godfather Float played a crucial role in the development of Boston's breaking scene from the mid-1980s to the mid-1990s, and I regard him as a primary inspiration and mentor. Unfortunately, his influence came to a halt when he encountered legal troubles and had to flee from the feds. Although he was close friends with my dad, they had to distance themselves due to Float's predicament, which impacted the dance's tutelage and created a ripple effect in our region's breaking community. In 1995, Float received an eleven-year prison sentence, further hindering his ability to contribute to the breaking scene. Nevertheless, the breaking scene in NYC and the northeast region experienced a resurgence in the mid-1990s, coinciding with Float's absence.

Float was widely considered one of the all-around b-boy kings in the elite class of breaking greats. Float's early mentors in the dance were Kid Freeze, a master of power/spin moves, and Fast Break, a master of footwork and freezes. Through his upbringing on the Lower East Side of NYC, Float developed a love for music that drove his passion for the craft.

Not only was he a b-boy king but also a well of wisdom. Speaking with my godfather, Float, felt like conversing with Yoda from *Star Wars*. Whenever I called him, I knew I had to prepare for an insightful conversation that would easily last over an hour. His spirit was humble, and his knowledge extended far beyond dance, touching on all aspects of life. Float overcame countless challenges, including being kidnapped as a child, surviving gunshots, serving time in prison, and battling cancer. Yet, through it all, he always made the most of his time on this earth.

• Visiting Float at the Federal Correctional Complex Allenwood in Allenwood, PA (2002).

Float's resilience and positivity in the face of adversity were truly inspiring. During his time in prison, he immersed himself in self-help books, always eager to share his newfound knowledge with others. He also DJed for fellow inmates using his radio and received mixtapes of 1980s NYC dance classics to practice and vibe to. Float became a familiar sight dancing on the handball courts, where he not only mastered but also innovated every aspect of the dance.

Float approached every interaction with an open heart and a genuine desire to uplift those around him. Whether mediating disputes between family or offering words of wisdom to young dancers, Float was a beacon of kindness and understanding. It's rare to find individuals in Hip Hop culture who are not only incredibly skilled but also grounded and caring. His legacy stands as a shining example of how the simple act of caring can inspire others and bring about positive change.

THE FLOORLORDS

• Promo press photo of the Floor Lords (1992).

In addition to Float, I learned from Floor Lords members Flex, Archie, and Lefty, who kept the dance alive in Boston when breaking lost popularity in the late 1980s. I observed their character and showmanship to learn the most. Flex and Lefty were always joking and sparring, while Archie would be in the corner, vibing to the music. They became the best by battling, performing, learning other dance styles, and staying true to themselves. They were genuine students of the craft and continued to learn and try new dance styles even as they got older.

Flex was a master of breaking, especially when it came to power moves, which he executed effortlessly. But what set him apart was his personality. He was the jester of the crew, always cracking jokes and keeping the vibe light even in the most stressful situations, such as shows or practice. As the rookies in the crew, my cousins and I were often the target of his hazing. After finishing a routine during a performance, Flex would often give us a playful slap on the head with his big ring, or cocotaso, or kick us in the butt as we walked onstage. Although it could be frustrating at times, we knew he was doing it in good spirits, to push our buttons and take us out of our comfort zones.

During one show, my cousin Ryno got hit with a playful cocotaso and started crying while performing a routine with El Nino and me. Even though we were just kids, we never complained about it. We thought it was all part of the process, a way of paying our dues to the crew.

Archie was a multitalented Hip Hop artist and one of the greatest b-boys from our region. Not only could he break with exceptional skill, but he could also rap and DJ and was a style king. His hand gestures were the most stylish while dancing and he always dressed to impress. Although he was a beast with his moves on the floor, what inspired me the most was his approach on top. He infused the late 1980s and early 1990s Hip Hop party dancing with his top rock and added his unique flavor to his steps. He was ahead of his time with his musicality in dancing, and his passion for music carried over to everything he did.

Every time he would spend the night over at my dad's house, he would head straight to the back room where all the records were. Whenever he DJed at my dad's house, he would let me sift through the record crates and choose which records to play for the mixtapes he would create. This experience played a significant role in shaping me as a DJ later on. Archie was always willing to share his knowledge of Hip Hop with my cousins and me, and I am forever grateful for that.

Lefty's martial arts discipline permeated every aspect of his life, including his breaking. Despite his age, he continued to improve because of his dedication to physical fitness and rigorous training. He also happened to be one of the great martial artists in Boston. When my cousins and I expressed interest in his fighting techniques, Lefty welcomed us into his gym. We were the only children in a room full of adults, but he put us through the same grueling drills and sparring sessions. That was our first and last day of serious martial arts training.

My uncles from the Floor Lords had a unique approach to guiding us in breaking. They treated us as equals, never viewing us as typical children. This mindset not only helped us prepare for life's challenges but also fostered our transition into adulthood from an early age. Though their unconventional style came with its challenges, growing up and dancing alongside my uncles from the Floor Lords was an invaluable experience.

Being around the Floor Lords didn't just shape my perspective on breaking; it also connected me to the broader movement of Hip Hop culture. Their stories and experiences introduced me to the larger ecosystem of dancers, DJs, and MCs who were keeping the culture alive beyond our local scene. This connection became even more evident in the 1990s, when Hip Hop experienced a powerful resurgence on the East Coast.

The East Coast Resurgence

In the 1990s, Hip Hop culture in its entirety experienced a resurgence in New York City. This was thanks in large part to events like the Universal Zulu Nation Anniversary and Rock Steady Crew Anniversary, which brought together people from all over the world to celebrate the various elements of Hip Hop. These gatherings provided a space for conscious thinking and creativity and were a welcome change from the negative portrayal of Hip Hop in the mainstream media. Members of the Floor Lords would attend these events and rave about the weekends and the talented performers they encountered.

As the Hip Hop community continued to thrive in New York City, we were fortunate to obtain VHS video tapes featuring high-level b-boys from around the world, thanks to connections made at events like the Universal Zulu Nation Anniversary and Rock Steady Crew Anniversary. Through trading with other practitioners, we acquired videos of Battle of the Year in Germany, B-boy Storm, Ken Swift, B-boy Summit, Jam on the Groove, and many other events, providing a valuable resource for me to study and learn from.

Crazy Legs is a legendary figure in Hip Hop culture and his Rock Steady Crew Anniversary festival was one of the most highly regarded events of its kind. The festival's reputation extended far beyond breaking because he had an impressive network of contacts in the Hip Hop community. He would bring in major acts from all elements of the culture, drawing diverse crowds to the festival. Before this time, I had never seen people from all over the world in a room breaking together, intertwined with pioneering DJs spinning, legendary MCs rocking the mic, and iconic style writers filling black books with fresh pieces. His ability to connect people beyond the breaking community was unmatched, reflecting his deep commitment as a culturalist of Hip Hop.

Looking back, attending NYC Hip Hop events in the late 1990s provided me with a solid Hip Hop foundation to build upon. Thanks to my dad's extensive network, I was fortunate to have deep connections in the mecca of Hip Hop culture. Meeting and seeing many of my childhood heroes at a young age, including Big Pun, Fat Joe, Big L, The Beatnuts, Kool Herc, and Grandmaster Caz, among other legends, was a classic experience. Prior to attending the Rock Steady Crew Anniversary in 1997, I had only seen these larger-than-life figures on TV or heard them on the radio. The event inspired me and made me feel like I could achieve greatness, just like these Hip Hop icons who came from similar backgrounds and upbringings in the hood.

I recall my first Rock Steady Crew Anniversary, packing into a fifteen-passenger van with the newer and older generations of the Floor Lords for the three-and-a-half-hour drive from Boston to the Bronx. It was a historic moment for our crew, as it marked the first time we traveled together outside of New England. As we approached our destination, Gaelic Park, the sound of boom-bap drums grew louder and louder. My dad led us around, greeting a few people wearing Zulu Nation medallions along the way. It was then that I saw Dave from the Boogie Brats dancing on the grass, executing four 1990 spins flawlessly. I was immediately impressed, and it was my first introduction to the Boogie Brats.

• Boogie Brats, Floor Lords, and Full Circle at Rock Steady Anniversary in Manhattan, NY (1997).

The Boogie Brats from Toronto were like big brothers to me, and I always felt their love and support. Their attitude toward the dance and their ability to get into the zone were a huge inspiration for me. The fact that there were three brothers in the crew reminded me of my cousins and me, but they were like an older version of us. I'll never forget the first time I saw them all get down together at Foretta's, a legendary practice spot in Manhattan, back in 1997. They took over the circles and danced with an intensity and style that I had never seen before. That night, the Boogie Brats changed my whole perspective on breaking.

• Boogie Brats in Toronto, Canada (1997).

Photo: Frank Boogie

During the late 1990s, breaking practitioners in NYC had a classic approach to the dance, with most of them mastering foundational footwork and a few moves. In contrast, breakers on the West Coast were focused on power moves. Yet the Boogie Brats had a unique approach that combined classic foundation with a twist. They incorporated threads, creative freezes, unorthodox transitions, and bits of power moves, footwork, and new patterns into their breaking style, which they called "origami."

Their style was something that the breaking scene had not witnessed in years prior. It looked as if you were watching footage in reverse, which I later learned was because they actually studied their footage in reverse to create some of their movements. This approach inspired me to rethink my own style and consider how I could turn everything upside down, incorporating head and neck transitions, movements, and threads in reverse.

I admired the Boogie Brats for their confidence, competitiveness, and unapologetic attitude, which they incorporated into their dance. They were never afraid to express how they felt about other b-boys or their breaking skills. One can understand their passion for breaking by watching the famous clip on YouTube of Megas and Kmel battling in a hotel hallway. It was always better to have them on your side than against you.

What set the Boogie Brats apart was their unique approach to breaking, which had a global impact despite their limited participation in competitions. They attended events to represent themselves in circles and rarely battled in competitions outside of Toronto. Their breaking style was in sync with the music, a quality not often found in most b-boys at the time. Arguably, as a collective, the Boogie Brats were among the rawest and most innovative b-boys of their generation.

To my surprise, I discovered that Frank Boogie, the popper of the Boogie Brats crew, had passed down valuable insights about musicality to his crewmates. As a popper, Frank was particularly attuned to the music, and he had learned from the legendary Electric Boogaloos how to use isolated movements to dissect the beats. The Boogie Brats incorporated this knowledge into their breaking, taking the dance to a new level of musicality and creativity.

In my opinion, Kmel of Boogie Brats (originally from NYC) is one of the greatest b-boys of all time. He has demonstrated mastery of every platform and style of breaking, from ciphers to competitions to the Hollywood industry. Kmel has earned the respect and admiration of breaking icons across generations and borders. Being in the presence of and eventually getting down with Boogie Brats in 2008 gave me confidence in my skills, knowing that I had some of the illest practitioners in breaking on my side.

• Incredible Breakers & Powerful Pexter in NYC (Early 1990s).
Photo: Incredible Josh

After attending the Rock Steady Anniversary in 1997, I returned to NYC the following year and had the opportunity to spend valuable time with the Incredible Breakers. I consider these veterans to be like my uncles, as they played a pivotal role in the growth and development of breaking within both my crew and the Boston scene in the 1990s. Their dynamic energy, commanding presence, and captivating stories from the 1980s breaking scene served as a great source of inspiration for me. The Incredible Breakers consisted of talented dancers such as Float, Chino, Bryant, Peanut, Nasty Nes, Awesome Paul, Sammy, Tiny, German, Incredible Josh, and others. Although there was limited footage of them during their active years, their reputation certainly preceded them.

Many seasoned breaking veterans spoke highly of Float, Chino, and Bryant, who were considered breaking gods due to their formidable challenges against numerous well-known breaking crews in NYC during the mid-1980s. Their approach to breaking greatly influenced my crew's dance style, particularly after their epic battle against the Floor Lords in 1984 at Club California in Boston, where the Floor Lords were outmatched and defeated. From that point on, my crew became dedicated students of the Incredible Breakers' philosophy on breaking.

The Incredible Breakers were famous for their powerful move combinations and top styles, but they didn't stop at mastering those aspects of breaking. I realized their dance level was due to their passion for music, which they imparted to us by teaching us that every element of breaking should be in sync with the music, even power moves. They had experienced the legendary NYC nightlife of Studio 54, The Funhouse, The Roxy, Roseland Ballroom, and countless other venues in the early 1980s, ensuring their expertise in dance and music was top-notch. They had a love for funk, soul, disco, Latin freestyle music, and Hip Hop.

• Incredible Breakers in the Bronx, NY (1984).

From the late 1990s to the mid-2000s, almost every summer weekend, we made the pilgrimage to Kingsbridge in the Bronx to learn breaking from the Davila family. Much like my own family, every member of the Davila Family danced, from the grandmother to the five brothers, sister, and nephew Incredible Josh. Sammy, Chino, Bryant, Eddie Ed (RIP), and their relatives warmly welcomed us into Sammy's living room, where he would play some of his favorite records on the turntable. We danced all night to classics like Atmosfear's "Dancing In Outerspace," C.J. & CO.'s "Devil's Gun," Babe Ruth's "The Mexican," James Brown's "Give It Up Or Turnit A Loose," and Booker T. & The M.G.s' "Melting Pot."

The music energized us, but it also earned us complaints from the neighbors. The neighbors would be banging on his door or hitting the ceiling below because we were dancing after midnight. The Davila's would either cuss back at the neighbors or ignore it while continuing to dance in true New York fashion. I looked at them like they were crazy, but it was still funny because I only witnessed this type of energy when I went to NYC. I got my first lessons on up-rocking from Sammy, Chino, Eddie Ed, and Bryant.

The Davila Brothers played a crucial role in my dance education, especially in improving my up-rocking. At one point, I was the weakest dancer in my crew when it came to dancing on top, but the Davilas guided and drilled me with new burns and rocking steps every time I visited them. I practiced what they taught me for hours at home and was determined to show them my progress. After weeks of training with the Incredible Breakers, I became one of the better up-rockers in my crew and in Boston.

By immersing myself in the Davilas' environment of soulful dancing and passion for music, I learned the essence of breaking. These experiences shaped not only my dancing but also my understanding of myself and my place in the culture. Though life was challenging, breaking became my way of channeling those struggles into something meaningful.

The Davilas always stole the show at our Floor Lords Anniversaries, despite being older than most of the crowd. Their infectious energy filled the room in a way I had never experienced. Their excellence in dance inspired my cousins and me to strive for greatness, and to this day, they remain the best b-boys of all time in our circle.

My inspirations from the 1990s instilled in me a deep respect for the culture and history behind breaking. Through their teaching and example, I learned not just the moves and techniques of breaking, but also the philosophy and values of the art form. They taught me that breaking is not just a hobby, but a way of life that requires discipline, humility, and respect. I carry with me the lessons and memories of this innovative time. Being studious is key to growth.

Mentorship Is Key

"When the student is ready, the teacher will appear. When the student is truly ready, the teacher will disappear." The origin of this quote is often debated, but its meaning has always resonated with me, especially when it comes to mentorship. Throughout this book, I acknowledge key individuals who have guided me, both directly and indirectly, in Hip Hop and in life. My mentors include my father, mother, grandmother Orfelina, Float, the Floor Lords, the Boogie Brats, the Incredible Breakers, Kon, Ken Swift, Leacy, Paulskeee, Timber, Forrest Getemgump, Lego, and Mex. Each of them has played a role in shaping who I am as a dancer and as a person, and I'm forever grateful for their influence.

Mentorship isn't talked about enough in Hip Hop culture. I don't see as many younger dancers actively seeking it today the way I did when I was coming up. At the same time, I've noticed that some breakers, after reaching a champion level, assume they no longer need guidance from those who helped them get there. It's natural to outgrow a mentor, but breaking, being such an individualistic and competitive art form, sometimes discourages dancers from continuing to learn from others. In other fields, whether it's music, sports, or martial arts, mentorship is often a lifelong pursuit.

Finding a mentor isn't always easy, and sometimes the right ones show up when you least expect them. But if you stay open, put in the work, and approach learning with sincerity, guidance will find its way to you. The key is to stay receptive.

As a student, earning the trust of a mentor requires discipline, humility, and consistency. If they see that your intentions are genuine, that you're not just looking for quick shortcuts but truly committed to the craft, they'll be more inclined to share their wisdom. And mentorship isn't a one-way street. I've always tried to give back in some form, whether through energy, time, or exchange. A balanced relationship makes mentorship stronger.

One thing I learned early on is that there's no single way to learn. While my elders had valuable lessons to share, I also had to discover my own path. Not every student absorbs information the same way, and I wish I had communicated that to my mentors more. The traditional way of teaching in breaking was often tough, with little consideration for different learning styles. Some people need to see, others need to hear, and some need to physically experience a movement over and over. Many of my elders didn't recognize this, and I sometimes felt the pressure of living up to their expectations. Looking back, I realize that their teaching style may have been shaped by their own experiences growing up in NYC in the 1970s and 1980s, a time and place that demanded resilience.

Even with great mentors, the dynamic isn't always perfect. Some mentors struggle to let go, even when their students have developed their own style or direction. A good mentor understands that growth sometimes means learning from new sources. My dad and Paulskeee instilled that in me early on, that I should learn from others too. The foundation they gave me allowed me to fully explore Hip Hop, and in doing so, I discovered my own creative identity. While my mentors shaped my journey, it was through immersing myself in all aspects of Hip Hop that I truly found my own voice.

CHAPTER 3

ALL HIP HOP ELEMENTS ARE RELEVANT

I believe that learning and incorporating all elements of Hip Hop gave me the tools to be creative and find my identity. I grew to respect the history of each art form and apply it to my life. To succeed in the Hip Hop arts, it's crucial to be culturally sound and open-minded. My advice to serious students is to seek knowledge from elite masters, practice, experience, innovate, and pass it down to the next generation. A strong foundation in Hip Hop culture can lead to greater artistic sense, networking opportunities, and the ability to move through different circles. This is the power of being culturally relevant in Breaking, DJing, Emceeing, and Writing.

• World Breaking Classic in Rotterdam, Netherlands (2011).

Photo: Maurice van der Meijs

Writing

When I was young, my dad told me that even as a b-boy, I needed to have a hand style. A hand style is how you write the English alphabet stylistically, particularly for your moniker (tag) in the art of aerosol writing. This type of writing is commonly referred to as "graffiti." But just like "breakdancing," it's the incorrect term the main-stream media uses to describe this art form. I learned about this art form and the importance of style through the teachings of PHASE II (RIP), known as the "father of style" and a Hip Hop renaissance man.

Growing up on the east coast, I was surrounded by impressive tags and pieces that inspired me. In the late '90s, my dad introduced me to the style writing pio-neers PHASE II and Vulcan, calling them "the best writers in the world." I was in awe. Learning later that they were rarely seen in public only deepened their mys-tique and my admiration for them.

It's surreal to think I was surrounded by a league of legends. Fifteen years after first meeting PHASE II, Paulskeee sent me a letter from him, reminding me of that childhood encounter. That moment brought everything full circle, and I'm grateful to have connected with such iconic figures in aerosol art.

• PHASE II Mike Dream (RIP) dedication (2000).
Photo: Paulskeee

Inspired by pioneers like PHASE II, Click rose as one of Boston's most influential writers in the 1980s and 1990s, renowned for his legendary pieces and exceptional lettering skills. My dad befriended him, and his mural in Peter's Park in the South End, right across from Boston City Lights, was pivotal to my artistic development. It was my earliest reference for understanding letter symmetry, color schemes, charac-ters, style, and message. The mural was a powerful symbol of the cycle of drugs and violence within Boston, and how it keeps Black and Brown men in prison. Through that piece, Click helped me realize that having a profound message behind your art is essential to educate people.

• Click @ Peters Park in Boston, MA (1990s).

Around the same time, I loved watching *Style Wars* (1983), a documentary about aerosol writing. I found the writers' personalities intriguing, like Kase2 (RIP), Skeme, and Dezzy Dez aka DJ Kay Slay (RIP). I always daydreamed about becoming a writer and feeling larger-than-life, like the writers in *Style Wars*. My first personal interaction with aerosol writing was hanging out with my cousins Flight and J-Quest. They were into writing just as much as they were into breaking, with black books filled with pieces and pictures of the pieces they had done around Boston. In elementary school, I would frequently tag my name "Lino" all over my notebooks, trying to mimic my older cousins.

One night, when Flight wasn't home, my cousins El Nino, Ryno, and I took his spray cans and went on a mission to tag up all around Humboldt Avenue in Dorchester. We knew we were up to no good, but the adrenaline rush we got from leaving our mark on the neighborhood was incredible. The next afternoon I felt an addiction to that adrenaline rush. There was a garage next to my grandmother's house that the local writers used to "get up" on. El Nino warned me that we shouldn't tag during the day, as it was too risky.

• Hanging with my cousins El Nino and Gio at the Piano Factory (1990s).

Common sense wasn't so common to me. So, I was caught up in my own hype and convinced my cousins to do it anyway. El Nino, Ryno, and I were about to tag the garage when the neighbors caught us red-handed as we entered through their fence. They yelled, "There they are! We finally caught these little bastards!" We were scared for our lives and didn't bother running. The neighbors immediately grabbed us by our shirts and threatened to call the police if we didn't tell them where we lived. My heart dropped.

We walked to El Nino's house in shame, terrified that my aunt Nancy or my dad would find out. We were teary-eyed, thinking we were about to catch the whooping of our lives. We breathed a sigh of relief as El Nino's sister Kimberly answered the door and none of our parents were home. Luckily, they just gave us a warning and didn't press charges against us.

Shout out to my cousin Kimberly for not ratting us out. She just yelled, "Don't y'all ever do that again! Next time I will tell Mami about this!" I took that experience in and never tagged anything illegally again. That was the first and only warning I needed. I gave up on my *Style Wars* dreams after that situation.

While I love writing and its characters, the lifestyle of an aerosol writer was too risky and dangerous. I stuck to the pen and paper and left it at that. To this day I still find inspiration from writers like PHASE II, Vulcan, Kase2, Click, Kem, Totem II, Teal, Can Two, Doves, Ces, Sofles, Bakeroner, Bates, and Revok. I appreciate writing just as much as any other Hip Hop element thanks to my dad and older cousins' guidance. Writing was my introduction to understanding aesthetics and style, not just in art, but in life.

• Lean Rock by Click (2013).

Emceeing

As aerosol writers paint the message, the MC speaks the message. Onyx was the first rap group that truly inspired me, and they were easily one of the most hardcore rap groups out during that time. Nothing got me more hyped than hearing Onyx's "Throw Ya Gunz" on the radio. Early in my dance career, I approached battling the same way Onyx approached rapping, with raw, aggressive, and hard-hitting energy. Onyx had some of the most intense beats and lyrics of their time. With violence rampant in my neighborhood during the 1990s, their music spoke to the environment I lived in.

I idolized Sticky Fingaz from Onyx so much that I remember going to the barbershop at five years old and demanding, "Shave my head like Sticky Fingaz!" The barber didn't follow my orders, so I was upset with him. When my dad walked over, the barber explained the situation, "Your son wants me to cut all his hair off like Sticky Fingaz." My dad laughed and replied, "Don't listen to that little guy. He's a maniac." Though I never shaved my head bald like Onyx did on the *Bacdafucup* (1993) album cover, I always made sure to imitate their mean mugs whenever I posed for a picture.

• My Sticky Fingaz expression (1993).

Two decades later, I had the chance to fulfill one of my childhood dreams, performing as a guest DJ for Onyx at the Legits Blast Festival in Slovakia (2017), in front of thousands of people. It was a last-minute opportunity since their DJ didn't show up, and I didn't even get to rehearse the show with them. Watching Sticky Fingaz on stage, I had to get all the cues from him on the fly. These guys seemed just as hardcore in real life as they were in their songs, so I couldn't afford to mess up their performance. Despite my nerves, we rocked the show and they gave me a lot of props for taking up the opportunity and handling it like a pro. That moment felt like destiny, and I'm sure that at some point in my childhood, I had prayed for it.

The 1990s was a heavy era for mixtapes in the rap game as it was the prime way for artists to gain exposure before signing with a major label. Alongside Onyx, my dad introduced me to the sounds of legendary Hip Hop DJs such as DJ Tony Touch, DJ Clue, DJ Juice, and Doo-Wop, as well as DJ Cash Money, among countless others. I would intently observe the mixes and analyze the tracklists to deepen my understanding of the music.

My dad also had a collection of iconic albums on heavy rotation, including Nas's *Illmatic*, Pete Rock & CL Smooth's *Mecca and The Soul Brother*, A Tribe Called Quest's *Midnight Marauders, Enter the Wu-Tang 36 Chambers, De La Soul Is Dead*, and Dr. Dre's *The Chronic*. These albums played a significant role in shaping my musical taste later in life, and although I appreciate most rap music, I always had a particular affinity for hardcore rap of the 1990s. For me, the hard-hitting drums and the messages within the lyrics were the essence of the genre.

Growing up, I was fortunate to be around some of Boston's most respected MCs, including Edo G, TDS Mob, Akrobatik, 7L & Esoteric, and many others, who were all good friends with my dad. I often tagged along with my dad to performances, where I had the chance to break while rappers performed and, on occasion, even performed alongside them. Many of these shows took place at The Middle East, a legendary venue in Cambridge, Massachusetts, known for its punk and indie rap shows. The energy at these sold-out shows was electric and intimate, thanks to the venue's layout. Over the years, I also witnessed acts like Statik Selektah and Termanology take the stage at The Middle East. While I deeply appreciated rap music, I was more of an observer than a practitioner, never pursuing emceeing as a personal craft.

• Performing with Onyx in Slovakia (2017).

DJing

There would be no rapper without the DJ. In 1999, we performed "Floor Lore" at Northeastern University's Blackman Auditorium, with LL Cool J's "Get Down" blaring from the speakers. The crowd erupted as DJ Ninja B flawlessly cut and juggled the lyrics, "Ninja of rap the boss is back!" ending his set with body tricks on the turntables and a peace sign to the audience. In Boston, Ninja B is considered our Hip Hop DJ hero, and he was my first introduction to DJing. I remember visiting his house, which was a 1990s Hip Hop artifact heaven with Juice and Illmatic posters on the walls and records everywhere. We spent countless hours watching Ninja B cut up and mix records, and his passion for the art form greatly inspired me.

My dad was one of Ninja B's biggest supporters, and he often traveled with him to New York City for major DJ battles. During the 1990s in NYC things could escalate quickly at DJ battles. It was not the safest environment as there were a lot of goons and Hip Hop fanatics that attended the DJ battles. Ninja was usually the only white guy from Boston at these events in NYC. The legendary rivalry between the Boston Red Sox and New York Yankees carried over into Hip Hop culture. People made him an easy target considering these Hip Hop events catered explicitly to black and brown people from the hood.

My dad usually intervened with hecklers and set things straight, almost as if he were Ninja's bodyguard. It would get rowdy in this environment. Ninja B became a rival of the legendary DJ Roc Raida (RIP), and the two had some of the most intense DJ battles at the New Music Seminar in 1991 and 1992. Roc Raida was always the crowd favorite, making Ninja's job even harder. Despite losing both battles, Ninja gained respect for his skills and was recognized as one of Roc Raida's fiercest competitors. As a white guy trying to earn respect in Black culture, gaining respect from the people in the mecca was extremely difficult, but Ninja's skills spoke for themselves.

• Rob Swift, Roc Raida, and Ninja B in New York, NY (Mid 1990s).

Photo: Rob Swift

In the 1990s, I was too young to fully comprehend the complexity of Ninja's skills. But even then, I was in awe of his lightning-fast cuts and juggles on the turntables. Although I didn't pursue DJing right away, I developed a deep respect for the craft thanks to my dad's connections to legends like Ninja. As a teenager, I was fortunate enough to have access to my dad's turntables and records, and I began honing my own DJing skills.

CHAPTER 4

FINDING MUSIC THROUGH STRUGGLES

• With my sister Madelyn at her baptism (2003).

While my journey into DJing was unfolding, little did I know, a much more pivotal moment was on the horizon, one that would change my life forever. It was a hot summer day in 2002, and my dad and I were rushing to teach a breaking class at a middle school in Mattapan, Massachusetts. We took a left turn, and then suddenly, a loud crash. My sight went black, and the next thing I knew, my head had gone crashing through the windshield. The glass shattered into thousands of tiny shards, slicing into my skin and leaving scars that would remain with me for years to come.

As I tried to make sense of what had happened, I realized that I was covered in blood and struggling to breathe. The smoke from the crash had filled my lungs, and I thought I might choke to death right then and there. When the ambulance arrived, one of the paramedics instructed me to lie down on the sidewalk and hold his hand as tightly as possible. My adrenaline was surging to a level I had never experienced before, causing me to grip his hand so tightly that he shouted out in pain. I was furious toward the person who caused the accident.

After the paramedics checked me, they rushed me to the hospital. When I arrived, they brought me to a doctor's office, where the nurse wiped the blood from my face and picked the glass out of my forehead. She then put stitches near the inside corner of my right eye. I was angry and begged my dad to get me out of there. Due to the intense fear and PTSD caused by the accident, I felt uneasy being in a car. For years, I would grip the ceiling handle every time I was in one, fearing another crash.

After the accident, life went on, and our family was about to experience a joyful event. On August 9, 2002, my mom gave birth to my baby sister Madelyn. I remember feeling overjoyed to become a big brother and rushed to the hospital to see her and my mom. Having Madelyn in our lives lifted our spirits and brought us closer together as a family. But, as time passed, my mom and stepdad faced challenges with their work schedules and the need to pick up Madelyn from daycare before 4 p.m.

After considering my options, I made the decision to quit playing football in my sophomore year of high school. I wanted to help my mom and make her life easier, so I took on the responsibility of picking up and watching my sister after daycare for a few months. I found that helping my family was more important than any extracurricular activity. This experience taught me the value of sacrifice and putting the needs of others before my own.

After quitting football to help take care of my baby sister, I tried out for the basketball team and got cut. It was a devastating blow. Basketball was the only thing that made me enjoy living in Stoughton. In basketball, my biggest inspirations in life were Michael Jordan, Kobe Bryant, and Kevin Garnett. I aspired to be like them. Not making the team made me feel like a failure for the first time in my life.

My life revolved around homework and watching Madelyn. Having been so busy with extracurricular activities my entire life, I suddenly felt like I had nothing for myself. Once I quit sports, it became more apparent to me that my skin color was different from that of the other kids, which made me feel lonely and disconnected. With more time on my hands, I began overthinking everything. I felt indifferent because things weren't working out the way I had hoped.

As I tried to navigate these personal challenges, tensions were also growing in my family life. My world was crumbling around me, and I became tired of being caught in the middle of my parents' fights. One incident stands out in my memory: I had to miss a day of school to perform at a Floor Lords show, and my mom was not having it.

I had never skipped school in my life, but I was torn between both parents and always felt like I was losing. After every argument, one of my parents would end up upset with me. It bothered me because I rarely got in trouble at school and never with the law. I found myself wondering, "Can't they just appreciate that they had a well-behaved child?" My relationship with my parents wasn't great during that time.

• Playing basketball in the 7th grade (2001).

I could see my mom's relationship with her husband falling apart, and I knew it was coming to an end. The constant changes and ongoing issues weighed heavily on us, and I struggled to keep up. As a teenager, I just wanted to live my life and enjoy it, but I didn't recognize my triggers or understand how these experiences were shaping me. I had no concept of mental boundaries or self-care. I felt lost and as if I was failing at life.

Therapy

During my sophomore year of high school, both my mom and dad noticed that I was struggling and suggested that I try therapy. At first, I was resistant to the idea. There was a stigma attached to seeking help for mental health issues during that time, and I didn't want to be seen as crazy. To make it easier for me, my mom also started seeing a therapist. During my first session, I was extremely guarded and didn't reveal much.

It took me months to open up about my life, as I had pent-up emotions and feared my parents' reactions. They were both strict with me in different ways, and I didn't want to disappoint them or be seen as weak. The PTSD from the car accident and the isolation that followed made everything worse, leaving me trapped in my own thoughts. After several sessions, I finally opened up about what was happening in my mind, becoming less reserved with my feelings. The therapist helped me become more expressive and communicative, offering insights on how to move forward in my life. She encouraged me to play sports again and socialize more with my peers, helping me break out of the shell I had built around myself. Looking back, therapy guided me toward a better future and helped me develop invaluable skills for my adult life.

As I continued on my journey of self-improvement through therapy, I stumbled upon an unexpected source of comfort in music, which helped me pass the time and provided an outlet for my emotions. I delved deeply into the world of rare funk and breaks, becoming obsessed with discovering obscure records. While making money from competing and performing with my crew, I spent all my earnings on either records or sneakers.

The first record I remember buying was a funky jazz record by Barbara Thompson called *Jubiaba*, that DJ Leacy, my idol at the time, used to play. I remember the rush I felt when I finally tracked down a copy and realized that few people knew about it. Discovering a new passion for music helped me cope with the challenges I faced earlier. It taught me the value of pursuing my interests and gave me a sense of purpose during a difficult time.

I spent a lot of time surfing the web and trading music on apps like AOL Instant Messenger and Soulseek, sharing music with others. During the week, I would spend five to six hours a day after school searching for music to buy from online record shops. On weekends, I would go to record stores to dig. If you added up all the hours I spent doing this as a teenager, it was close to working a full-time job. Collecting records and learning about music became an escape for me, and I felt like I had found something new that fulfilled my competitive edge.

It was a rush for me because it was the one thing that made me feel like I was accomplishing something with my life. I experienced happiness whenever I found a dope song, and digging for music fed my soul and heart. It was about the journey of finding a record that I loved, whether it was something I was searching for or something I came across by chance. This was a special time in my life because, not only was I going to therapy, but I also found therapy through music.

Young Scholar

While music gave me a sense of accomplishment and fulfillment, school presented a different kind of challenge. I had always been a capable student, coasting through most subjects without much effort. However, that changed when I encountered Algebra II in my sophomore year. Being one of the few sophomores in a class full of juniors made me feel alienated, and I was uncomfortable with the subject because I ignorantly believed that math classes would not apply to my future life. It was like an alien language to me. Unfortunately, I received an F in Algebra II, which was the first time in my life that I had failed a class.

I was nervous and embarrassed to show my mom the failing grade, and I prepared myself for a verbal lashing. Surprisingly, her reaction was one of disappointment. I had let my mom down, and seeing her disappointment felt worse than getting yelled at. I couldn't bear to let that happen again and barely scraped by in my math courses.

Unlike Algebra II, History has always been one of my favorite subjects. Hip Hop culture taught me to appreciate history, honor my elders, and learn from the past. These values shaped my love for history classes. Growing up in Boston, a city rich with historical significance, I took pride in its legacy. Whether guiding visitors along the Freedom Trail or exploring the Paul Revere House, I found joy in sharing my city's past. This deep appreciation for history is ingrained in my culture and aligns with Hip Hop's philosophy of knowing and respecting one's roots. Because of this, I thrived in history classes.

In some ways, I knew what I wanted to do as a b-boy and DJ, but I did not have a clear academic pathway to get there. Although I loved Hip Hop, I had doubts about pursuing it as a career. Making a living as an artist is not easy, and I have seen many people struggle to do so through dance. Even successful dancers didn't always have financial stability. This reality discouraged me, making me wonder if I should pursue something more practical.

Despite my uncertainty, I applied to college, unsure of what to study or what career to pursue. My initial motivation came from wanting to make my mom proud, to show her that her sacrifices had not been in vain. I hoped college would help me find my path and give her a reason to be proud of me.

Though I understood my mom's concern about getting a formal education, I felt lost. Seeking my own path, I left Boston to attend Florida International University in Miami. Without scholarships, I relied on student loans to cover tuition, a tough choice given the cost. If I had completed all four years in Miami, my debt would have exceeded $100,000. That financial burden forced me to reconsider my future. While earning a degree seemed practical, I couldn't shake the feeling that my purpose lay elsewhere. That realization brought me back to breaking, something that had always been part of my life.

Conflicted to Be Great

Growing up around some of the most skilled breaking practitioners, I had a complicated relationship with Hip Hop. While I loved the art form, my heart wasn't fully in it. Breaking started as something fun, even though I knew I had the potential to be great. Following in the footsteps of a legendary lineage both pushed me to improve and weighed on me with its expectations.

The standards were sky-high, and I felt my dad demanded nothing less than perfection. I always felt the pressure to measure up to my dad, Float, Kmel, Incredible Josh, Flight, and El Nino. Failing to meet their expectations left me feeling disappointed. Still, I continued to pursue breaking, determined to find my place within the culture. Though it wasn't easy, I eventually discovered a deeper connection to the art and the passion needed to succeed.

The move to the suburbs profoundly impacted my relationship with Hip Hop, more than I could have imagined. My mom didn't approve of the Hip Hop lifestyle, and a part of me didn't either. Without my cousins immersed in the scene, I struggled to find my footing. Watching my dad and crewmates work hard yet still struggle financially only deepened my doubts.

During the late 1990s–2000s, society was much more against Hip Hop, and there were limited opportunities for breaking. I remember feeling lost and unsure about my passion for Hip Hop, which was once so strong. It felt like a distant dream, and I struggled to reconcile my love for it with the realities of suburban life. I longed for the sense of community and connection that came with Hip Hop, but it seemed out of reach.

Dealing with the inner conflict of whether or not to pursue breaking was a constant struggle for me. My cousins were committed to becoming the best, and I wasn't. They trained every day and pushed each other to be the best, while I held back due to fear and self-doubt. It didn't help that my dad would compare me to them, making me feel insecure. But as I got older, I realized that I had to take ownership of my own journey.

It wasn't until my late teenage years that I committed to becoming better at the dance. I started traveling to Boston on my own to practice and gain clarity on my dancing goals. It wasn't easy practicing alone, but I pushed myself harder than ever before. Through perseverance and dedication, I finally found my confidence in breaking, and it became a true passion that I couldn't imagine living without. At the same time, my love for DJing was growing, and the two became inseparable.

CHAPTER 5

THE PATH OF
DJ LEAN ROCK

One of my earliest memories of digging for music was when my dad took me to re-cord stores on Newbury Street in Boston and then to Traffic Entertainment Group's warehouse. As we walked through the building, I saw rap posters of the Fat Boys from the 1980s, holy grail MF DOOM merchandise, and boxes of reissued rap re-cords. After my dad talked with one of his friends in one of the offices, we headed to the back of the warehouse looking for records.

The first records I looked through were a collection of 45 reissues or new funk 45s by indie record labels such as Funk 45, Daptone Records, Kay Dee Records, and Stark Reality. These labels were known for producing high-quality funk and soul music, and I was excited to discover new and unique sounds from their collections. I played the records on the listening station and explored to find a break that I had not heard before. This was the beginning of my interest in digging for music, which involved helping my dad find records to play at local jams or for his mixtapes. Going record-digging for the first time was an exhilarating experience.

I didn't own a turntable in Stoughton, but that didn't stop me from helping my dad find the next gem. He had DJ equipment and a bunch of records in the back room of his apartment, and I would go to the DJ room in the morning and play re-cords from my dad's collection. Although I started collecting records for myself, my main motivation was the love of great music for breaking.

To fuel my obsession, I relied on seven key websites where I would religiously search for records or sound bites: Funk45.com, Allmusic.com, eBay, Gemm.com, MusicStack, CDandLP.com, and Recordkingz.com. Each site offered unique resourc-es that helped me find the rarest and most sought-after tracks. I became obsessed with the hunt for obscure funk and breakbeats.

Despite my dad's encouragement to pursue DJing, I initially hesitated because I didn't think my personality suited the job. East Coast DJs were known for their strong presence on the mic, but I lacked the proper articulation, voice, or charisma and was terrified of public speaking. Nonetheless, my love for digging for music persisted and I found joy in sharing my finds with friends. It was a personal aspect of the music scene that I felt connected to, even if DJing didn't feel like the right fit for me.

After a few years of digging, four pivotal events forever changed my life: meeting DJ Kon of Kon and Amir in 2003, the passing of DJ Leacy in 2004, my first opportunity to DJ at Ken Swift's "Raiders of the Lost Art" event in Boston in 2005 and attending Out For Fame Bronx that same year to build with Paulskeee. These experiences deepened my appreciation for the art of DJing and I am forever grateful for the influence and impact of DJ Kon, DJ Leacy, Ken Swift, and Paulskeee. Their passion and dedication continue to inspire me today, and I am honored to have learned from and worked alongside them. These are my flowers to these highly influential individuals.

• With DJ Kon at the Middlesex in Cambridge, MA (2022).

DJ Kon

In the summer of 2003, my dad took me to DJ Kon's house to learn and discover rare records. I had been to many DJs' houses before, but Kon's record collection was on another level. It was a big collection, and all the records were high-quality. He had thousands of records organized and a few just lying around. Some of the first records I spotted in his DJ room were Mulatu Astatke's *Mulatu of Ethiopia*, Niagara's *S/T*, de Wolfe Music's *Hard Hitter*, The Stark Reality's *Discovers Hoagy Carmichael's Music Shop* album, and a few other holy grails.

At the time, I didn't know what these records were, but their covers immediately caught my attention. My dad had spoken highly of Kon for some time, so my expectations were high. Kon did not disappoint. He was welcoming and generous with his knowledge, allowing me to dig through his collection and teaching me about the artists and their music.

My dad brought DJ Leacy's *Breaksploitation* record with him and asked Kon if he recognized any of the breaks. Sure enough, Kon started pulling out all of the original records Leacy had used for that compilation. It blew my mind because, at the time, it seemed impossible to find any of the records Leacy played. I had only heard most of them on VHS tapes, his mixtapes, or online.

• Breaksploitation cover by Dan Lish for Break DJ Leacy (2002).

We were in the middle of the hood of Dorchester in our hometown, and there we were, listening to Kon play all of DJ Leacy's signatures and some mind-blowing breaks we'd never heard before. It was incredible to see him pull out obscure Italian library records, private-pressed disco records with breaks, and other grooves from Europe. Kon not only had one of the dopest record collections, but he was also a talented DJ and deeply passionate about music. Spending just a few hours at Kon's house opened my mind to a whole new dimension of music, and his musical ear inspired me to dig deeper than ever before.

• DJ Leacy at B-boy Masters Pro-Am in Miami, FL (2000).

Photo: Ervin Arana

DJ Leacy

DJ Leacy from London, England, was my first inspiration as a DJ who focused specifically on b-boys and b-girls. He coined the term "Break DJ" and gave me and many others a new lane for DJs to play. He was the number one DJ in the breaking community from the mid-1990s until he passed away in 2004. Leacy was the headlining DJ for all the bigger breaking events worldwide during that time, including Battle Of The Year, UK B-boy Champs, Pro-Am, Mighty4, and Freestyle Session.

Leacy's DJing changed my life forever. He elevated breakbeat music, introducing a new generation to classic tracks. His selections included breakbeat classics, classic Hip Hop, electro-funk, forgotten 1970s and 1980s breaks, rare British/Euro funk, and more. He had a unique talent for dropping a beat just for a dancer and changing the rhythm at the perfect moment, making his musical choices feel like scenes unfolding in a movie. In my opinion, Leacy is the greatest break DJ of all time.

Leacy was also known for introducing tracks that became staples in the breaking community. He traveled frequently between London and New York, studying the pioneers of Hip Hop and exploring the history of first and second-generation Hip Hop DJs. By reviving classic beats from the 1970s and 1980s, many of which were played at park jams but never included in the *Ultimate Breaks & Beats* compilation series, he brought those records back to the forefront at breaking events. His efforts helped keep the spirit of the original Hip Hop culture alive.

Everyone in my crew talked about how Leacy was the highlight of the Pro-Am event in Miami in 1999. It was the first time I'd ever heard a DJ receive such praise at a breaking event, especially with so many Hip Hop legends in attendance. My dad brought back Leacy's mixtapes, which quickly became my favorite break mixes. After practicing with them for a year, I finally got to experience my first live Leacy set at Pro-Am 2000, which also happened to be the first event I attended outside of the northeast region.

Pro-Am, organized by Speedy Legs and Zulu Gremlin, was one of the best Hip Hop events in the world, drawing people from all over to celebrate the culture. The event lasted three days, and Leacy likely brought close to a thousand records from London to Miami, putting in serious work on the turntables. During this era, DJs used vinyl. My dad was excited for El Nino and me to meet Leacy and personally introduced us, eager for us to connect with someone so influential in the scene.

Leacy was a tall, lanky guy who towered over us. Even in our brief conversation, he exuded a humble spirit and a deep passion for Hip Hop culture. He is one of the few people I've met who left me starstruck. People cheered for him playing breaks just as much as they cheered for the dancers, something I had never witnessed at a breaking jam before meeting Leacy.

I remember sitting to the right of Leacy with my crew during the battles, blown away by his track choices. One standout moment was when he played the Nite Liters' "Nothing" during B-boy Cloud's battle against Incredible Josh. The song's intro became iconic in that battle and came to be known as the "Theme from Cloud." I also vividly recall Leacy cutting up the break on Nina Simone's "Funkier Than A Mosquito's Tweeter" while Abstrak battled Benji. Abstrak's moves perfectly embodied the song's rhythm and beats. Thanks to Leacy's soundtrack, Pro-Am 2000 became one of the most incredible breaking events I've ever attended.

Then, on October 14, 2004, four years after that unforgettable weekend at Pro-Am, we were practicing when my dad received a frantic call. He told us the devastating news that DJ Leacy had passed away. We were all in shock and disbelief. The practice, which had been filled with energy and excitement moments before, became quiet and somber.

In honor of Leacy, we played the classic *20th Century Rock* mix that he had collaborated on with Ken Swift. I remember us dancing with our heads down in mourning. Looking back, it almost feels as though that mix, played in Leacy's memory, was a foreshadowing of the opportunity I would later receive to DJ at Ken Swift's jam.

• Celebrating my birthday with DJ Leacy on the wall (2020).

Photo: RoxRite

When I got home that night, the news hit me hard. I felt a profound sense of loss and sadness. It was a strange feeling because at the same time, I felt like something was calling me to continue Leacy's legacy. As I grieved, I realized that I had to step up and pick up the slack left by his passing. Before that day, DJing had never felt like my calling, but after hearing Leacy and Ken Swift's 20th Century Rock on repeat, I knew it was the path I was meant to take.

• With Ken Swift at Styles No Jokin in Los Angeles, CA (2019).

Photo: Adam Adolphus

Ken Swift

Ken Swift is a true embodiment of the b-boy ethos. His innovative style and unique approach to breaking have had a profound impact on my own development as a dancer. When I first met him at Rock Steady Anniversary, I was struck by his effortless cool: He had one pant leg rolled up, a fresh Adidas fit, and a hat tilted to the side. But it wasn't just his appearance that stood out. Even off the dance floor, Ken exuded a magnetic energy that drew people to him.

As I watched him dance during the crew performance, I was inspired by his commitment to precision and his emphasis on angles and stylized movements. From that moment on, I knew that I wanted to emulate his approach and incorporate it into my own breaking style. Kenny's footwork technique revolutionized the way practitioners approached breaking in the late 1990s. With his footwork, he was one of the first b-boys I had ever seen dissecting the music with speed and cadence.

While most people were breaking circularly (clockwise/counter), Kenny broke the flow and did footwork from every angle and direction, whether in the air, high or low to the ground. He utilized all the space on the floor with his movement, keeping you guessing with his freestyle approach. He evolved the moves he created in the 1980s in the 1990s, well into the 2000s, and even today. His footwork looked more dynamic than most people could do with power moves.

One of my favorite Ken Swift moments was watching him perform a solo round to Dennis Coffey's "Scorpio" during a Rock Steady show in Japan. His partner, Mr. Wiggles, acted like he was performing CPR with his hands on Ken Swift's chest on the beat. As Wiggles pressed Kenny's chest, the kick drum on the record sounded like a heartbeat. When the break dropped, Ken Swift came to life and went off on a footwork tangent remaining in the pocket with the music. Ken Swift had the perfect b-boy form and the best footwork I've ever witnessed, making that moment unforgettable. That ability to move with the music and embody the rhythm was something I always admired about Ken Swift.

So when I found myself unexpectedly DJing at his jam, *Raiders of the Lost Art*, on March 25, 2005, it felt surreal. Ken Swift had thrown the jam with my dad in Boston, and originally, DJ Forrest Getemgump was supposed to play. DJ Forrest Getemgump couldn't make it, and my dad was too busy to DJ the whole event, so he put me on as a last-minute change to fill in some time. I was nervously shaking because people only knew me as a b-boy, and I didn't know how they would react. I had just started practicing DJing a few months before the event. This was going to be the first jam I spun at, but it also happened to be Ken Swift's jam. In my head, this was the equivalent of having to DJ a party for Prince or Michael Jackson with no prior DJ experience.

While the event was smaller, I still had to make sure the iconic Ken Swift was satisfied with the music. I did pretty well for my first jam, and people recognized my potential. I was only using vinyl. Some older folks appreciated seeing a young DJ rock doubles of breaks on vinyl, as it was a rarity since most of the DJs that played breakbeats were much older than me. I loved the feeling of people coming up to me and saying, "Damn, kid! You're playing some dope shit!"

I appreciated that the people in my hometown were finally showing love, because I felt like the breaking scene in Boston hated my crew. It was great not to feel hostility and to feel some praise from other breakers. The music and DJing pushed me on a path of happiness. I was able to DJ at a few smaller events in Boston, slowly gaining confidence. While at school, I began writing down all the major breaking events I wanted to DJ at. I envisioned myself on those stages.

Paulskeee

Later that year, in December 2005, I began building with Paulskeee, a prominent Hip Hop event organizer and leader of the Rock Force Crew, at Jeskilz's apartment in Harlem before his Out For Fame Bronx event. Growing up, I had watched his event videos and noticed that he paid more attention to the music than any other promoter. As a curator, he selected DJs who were not only technically skilled but also had an impeccable musical selection, always playing the funkiest tracks.

I sparked a conversation with him about music at jams that day, seeking insight. I was surprised by his curiosity, despite our age difference. Paul was an open ear. While others chatted, I connected with him on breakbeats and my philosophy on music for breaking.

Later that evening, we headed to the jam at LPAC, a legendary venue in the Bronx. We had great memories of attending events there and were excited to return to the competitive NYC scene. After heavy training, we were determined to win Out For Fame Bronx. We breezed through most of the competition, but the final battle was close. Although we won, there was controversy surrounding the judges' decision to pick us over the hometown favorites. Many criticized Kmel's choice, unaware that he had initially voted for a tie, sparking a heated rivalry with NYC veteran Jiggz that would continue for the following year.

Amidst this, my perspective on DJing began to shift. While the crowd loved DJ Skeme Richards' set, I wasn't as impressed. I recognized many of the records and felt his selection was solid but nothing groundbreaking. When I shared this with Paul, his reaction made me pause. He explained that while I understood breakbeats at 16, I hadn't yet grasped the technical side of DJing, how presentation, crowd interaction, and subtle details could elevate a set. That insight stuck with me.

After connecting with Paul in NYC, I began sending him music through AOL Instant Messenger. He recognized my potential and offered mentorship in DJing, business, and networking. With his guidance, I learned how to market myself and gained confidence. He taught me to use the internet and social media to grow my platform.

Paul had a gift for inspiring those around him. The champions he trained were proof of that. He encouraged me to think beyond breaking and DJing, emphasizing the importance of connecting with people from different elements of Hip Hop and beyond. At his event, The Mighty4, you wouldn't just see breakers. You would see respected aerosol writers, MCs, DJs, educators, and other figures from the arts.

Paul brought together diverse crowds, health-conscious individuals, stylish partygoers, and grassroots organizers, creating a space for exchanging ideas and pushing the culture forward.

Beyond Hip Hop, Paul introduced me to strategic thinking. He shared books, articles, and documentaries that shaped my mindset. He introduced me to authors like Sun Tzu, Robert Greene, John Wooden, and Cal Newport, encouraging me to study strategy and politics, essentials for navigating the drama and competition in the breaking world. One day, he even took me to a bookstore and handed me *The 33 Strategies of War*. I remember thinking, "Damn, this is a lot to take in!" At first, the lessons felt abstract, but over time, they became clear, and I started seeing how they applied to battles, event organizing, and career moves.

Paul's understanding of strategy and politics fueled his deep knowledge of breaking and its history. While many had footage of breaking, few truly understood its cultural significance or evolution. Paul had an academic-like approach to breaking, interviewing pioneers and style masters worldwide, transcribing their insights into a system that facilitated efficient learning and training.

• Paulskeee at San Leandro High School in San Leandro, CA (2018).

Photo: Matt Hoang

Over time, I realized that Paul wasn't just an educator within Hip Hop. He was bridging the gap between culture and academia. As a high school teacher and college professor, he integrated Hip Hop's philosophy into structured education, a path few had explored. His ability to break down complex ideas and offer fresh perspectives was transformative. Through his mentorship, I was inspired to expand my role beyond DJing to becoming an educator myself. As I've grown in this role, I've gained a deeper appreciation for how various influences, whether individuals, crews, or cultural movements, have shaped breaking over the years.

The Horsepower DJs

In the mid-2000s, the global breaking scene began to shift toward competitive events, which became more prolonged due to excessive sign-up competitions for breakers. This shift brought about a demand for high-energy breakbeats that could fuel b-boys and b-girls to excel in battles. I realized I was onto something new in terms of unheard-of music that was missing from the American breaking scene. Most American break DJs weren't spinning library records, obscure Euro grooves, or privately pressed funk records from America.

During that era, I had an edge in rare funk music thanks to my network of fellow DJs. I frequently conversed with DJs such as Kon, Serge Gamesbourg (Boston), Popsicle (Boston), Just One (England), Chung (The Netherlands), Billy Brown (France), and Los Boogie (Minnesota), who shared their philosophy on DJing with me and sent music files and rare records my way. Thanks to their generosity and Recordkingz.com, I gained knowledge about rare records and unique covers of popular breakbeats. With every discovery of obscure music, it felt like I was accessing a new world of sound.

As my collection and understanding of breakbeats expanded, so did my drive to curate and play the best breaks. This passion naturally led to deeper connections with like-minded DJs. In 2005, DJ Timber and I started a DJ crew called Horsepower after a few conversations on email and MSN Messenger. We would call a dope break "Horse Power." Anything subpar of being dope would be called "Pony Power." This joke evolved into a real DJ crew, and we were eager to put our work out there and prove that the breaks we played were the best. I was already sharing music with two UK DJs, Timber and Just One. Since they were already friends, we decided to join forces. Timber and Just One were ahead of the game with their breakbeat selection. Their sets featured breakbeats with a hardcore, funky sound reminiscent of high-energy car chase music from blaxploitation films, giving dancers the drive and energy they needed.

• DJ Timber in Toronto, Canada (2020).

DJ Timber, originally from Ireland, is one of the most passionate DJs I have ever met when it comes to music. I have always loved his energy and the vibe he brings to the table. In my opinion, Timber was one of the illest break DJs of the mid-2000s.

I first emailed Timber because I was so inspired by his *Break Beast* mix that came out in 2005. I thought it was one of the most impressive mixes of that time because of its break selection. While I took pride in knowing many breaks, I did not recognize a lot of the songs he used. I emailed Timber about the tracks and asked if he would trade music with me, but he either shut me down or sent over fake track names.

I spent months hunting for those tracks on vinyl, only to realize they did not exist. In the process, I was discovering new breaks I had never heard before. Timber was schooling me without ever giving me a straight answer. He would laugh at my struggles, watching me chase ghost records for months, before finally giving up the real track names. He had a twisted sense of humor, but he knew I was serious about the music.

On April 16, 2006, I was scheduled to battle with the Floor Lords at Fresh Jive in Leeds, England. Before the event, I asked my dad to talk to the organizer and request that they hire DJ Timber. When I met Timber at the jam, he towered over me at 6 '4'' and greeted me with a friendly "What up, Shorty." I knew he would play some tunes that I had been asking him about.

The event was four hours away from London, so I didn't expect Just One to show up. However, he surprised me by coming to chill and even gave me a CD full of rare library breaks. I was thrilled about it because I knew there was serious heat on the CD.

When Timber hit the turntables, he went in. He started with a cover of Babe Ruth's "The Mexican" by Rare Bird, "Dollars." I had heard this record on his mixtape, but then he played a version I had never heard before. Then came a wild Moog version of *The Mexican* with an insane break in it, and I stood there in disbelief. Where was he finding these breaks? Each track hit harder than the last. It turned out he was working at Vox Pop Records, one of the best record stores in England at the time.

Timber's DJ style had a unique energy that introduced me to fresh, unheard covers of breakbeats. He did not rely heavily on technical scratching, but his beat selections were raw and invigorating. His music alone was enough to hype the room, and I even modeled aspects of my own style after his. Beyond his skills on the decks, I admired how he commanded attention just by being himself. He had a charisma that set the tone for the room, and he constantly educated breakers on understanding tempo and vibe, earning their respect through the music.

The mid-2000s were a unique era when the only way to hear certain songs was through mixtapes or live DJ sets. DJs kept their signature tracks a secret, setting themselves apart with exclusives. There was no Shazam and no YouTube deep dives. Finding certain records was a real challenge. Timber was one of the key figures keeping that culture alive, constantly digging and breaking records that most people could only dream of having.

As much as Timber was passionate about music, he also had a deep love for breaking. We took immense pride in not just DJing but stepping into the cipher ourselves. DJs hopping into the cipher was not something you saw often. It was rare for DJs to not just play the music but become the music. Timber and I made it a thing in the mid-2000s, showing that DJs could rock both the decks and the floor.

One of my fondest memories was DJing at the Floor Lords' 26th Anniversary celebration, where I jumped into the cipher with Timber and Forrest Gettemgump, another DJ who had a huge impact on me. The energy in that moment was unreal. Three DJs, breaking together while still controlling the music. It was a rare experience that reminded everyone in the room just how inseparable music and dance really are.

• DJ Forrest Getemgump in Ohio (2020).

Forrest Getemgump, my DJ big brother, played a significant role in shaping my career and the direction of the Horsepower DJs. His deep roots in Hip Hop and connection to its original lineage influenced our collective approach to music. He was a true student of the culture, respected by many of Hip Hop's architects and game-changers across all its elements. Gump was one of the most dedicated diggers of breakbeats, one of the best break DJs of the 2000s, and one of the few NYC b-boys who kept the spirit of breaking alive in the city during the 1990s.

His passion for Hip Hop culture was unparalleled, and he was always a stand-up guy, which is why so many people respected and loved him. Thanks to Gump, I had the opportunity to connect with and build relationships with heavy hitters like DJ Scratch, Spinna, Large Professor, and JBX of Big City Records. He was also close friends with DJ Leacy and was affiliated with First Nature at one point, solidifying his reputation as a break DJ.

Gump was always quick to give props and show respect to other legendary Hip Hop heads. He introduced me to the P Brothers, Rockin' Rob, Chuck City, and many more without ever making me feel like I should have already known them. Learning about these DJs was meaningful and inspired me to dig deeper and refine my skills as a DJ. He also helped me build relationships with many of these elders by publicly praising my work, which opened doors for me as one of the few younger DJs keeping the essence of Hip Hop alive through breakbeats.

Gump's dedication to discovering new music and his calm demeanor were just two of the many qualities that made him an invaluable mentor to me. I was so eager to learn from him that I would often take the bus from Boston to NYC just to soak up his knowledge. As wild as NYC was in the mid-2000s, Gump always remained composed, even in the most chaotic settings. His knowledge of the city's record stores was extensive, and he took me to some of the best spots for finding rare and classic records. Even when we found ourselves in strange or difficult situations, Gump stayed level-headed and had a way of making me feel at ease.

One memory that stands out is our visit to Beat Street Records in the Bronx. Gump had shared the story of how he and Leacy discovered John Davis' *I Can't Stop* 12-inch and Fred Karlin's *Up the Down Staircase* LP at his favorite record store, which made me eager to visit it myself. He loved the store for its rare finds, despite the owner's unpredictable and eccentric behavior.

The first and only time I visited the store with Gump, the owner decided to close up as soon as we arrived in the middle of the day. Frustrated, the owner snapped, "I'm closed!" Gump pleaded, "Come on, man, just let us in for a few." But the owner refused. As we drove off, we watched him kick McDonald's cups full of soda at cars on Jerome Avenue. It was classic Bronx behavior, and we couldn't help but laugh at how accurately Gump had described him. Despite the setback, we continued our hunt for the music we loved.

Our time in New York City during the mid-2000s was always centered around music. Whether we were digging all over the East Village, which was a record haven at the time, or hanging out at Big City Records, our mission was always the same: to track down the best b-boy breaks and funk records.

While I looked up to Gump as a mentor, I also had something to offer in return. I had access to certain records and information he wanted, and I was happy to share them out of respect for him. Gump was always generous with his knowledge, unlike some elders in Hip Hop who preferred to keep to themselves. Eventually, I invited Gump to be part of Horsepower, and he was proud to represent us.

Over time, I connected with like-minded DJs and formed strong bonds with Jus Jones from Hawai'i and Smokestack from Oakland. Their passion for music and dedication to the craft made them a perfect fit for Horsepower DJs. Together, we popularized a range of records in breaking, including *Sarabande* by Symphonic Metamorphosis, *Soul Entertainer* by Respect, *I Found Sunshine* by The Young Ideas, and *You're Hip, Miss Pastorfield* by Fred Karlin.

Having a DJ crew made the digging process much easier since we lived in different parts of the world and had access to records that others in our city, state, or country wouldn't have. With this advantage, we uncovered an incredible number of breaks and rare finds. Our collective vision was to bring the most aggressive, rare, and hardest breakbeat drums the scene had ever heard.

The Horsepower sound sparked a revival of traditional breakbeats but with a fresh, hard-hitting edge. The breaking community was highly competitive, and other DJs constantly pushed us to innovate. Through collaboration and an international network of like-minded DJs, we stayed ahead of the curve and introduced new music that filled a void in the breaking scene. At the time, most DJs had a regional sound, but we shared music across borders, creating something truly unique.

While many DJs contributed to this movement, Horsepower stood out for its ability to connect and collaborate across regions. Our passion and dedication to the craft had a significant impact on the global breaking scene from 2005 to 2012. In my opinion, those were the golden years for breakbeat DJs and competitive breaking. I don't recall another time when there were so many talented break DJs. During those years, we expanded our crew to include Woo-d from Slovenia, Kogataroo from Japan, DJ Shame from Massachusetts, and DJ Kidragon from San Diego.

Despite the age difference, with me being the youngest member and everyone else ten to twenty years older, we worked together to create music that elevated breaking competitions and Hip Hop culture. Looking back, it's crazy to think that at just sixteen, I was leading and organizing the crew without even realizing it.

As people's priorities shifted, the crew eventually faded out. But Horsepower played a vital role in my career, and I'm grateful for the experiences and lessons that came with it. I believe God connected me with these DJs to help influence a new generation of dancers.

• Horsepower logo design by Dwelz (2008).

Becoming A National Breaking Champion

As my DJing career gained momentum, I continued to compete in breaking competitions with my crew. In 2006 we were preparing for the Out For Fame US National
Final in San Francisco, the most prominent national championship in breaking at
the time, featuring the eight best crews in the nation. After months of practice, we
were finally on our way to San Francisco for the first time, with a six-hour early
morning flight and no sleep. Our goal was to become the youngest national breaking champion crew, with most of us aged fifteen to seventeen years old.

We were excited to compete on the West Coast and eager to show what we could
do. Before this trip, I only knew a few things about San Francisco: my mom's birthplace, *Full House* (TV show), Rock Force Crew and Renegades (breaking crews), the
49ers, the Giants, and the famous hills of San Francisco. I had been to LA two years
prior, but it seemed San Francisco was a much safer city based on our arrival. I never heard anything about San Francisco being dangerous or even having any gangs.

The Friday before the championship we got picked up from the airport and went
straight to our hotel. My dad's friend gave us directions to take the Bart train and get
off at 16th and Mission where he would pick us up. We washed up, changed clothes,
and headed to Cellspace SF for the pre-party. My dad and I, El Nino, Lil Dee, and
Heat Rock were hanging out, waiting to take the Bart train with my dad. We had
been practicing for months and were excited to show off our skills in the circles.

As we boarded the train, we noticed a higher than usual number of homeless
people, but we didn't think much of it. At 16th St. Mission Station, we got off and
a young Latino kid rushed past us with an unsettling energy. We couldn't quite put
our finger on what was off, but it made us feel uneasy. My dad called his friend to
see where he was, and he said he'd be running a bit late. He told us to wait on the
corner outside the station, and he'd pick us up when he arrived.

As we walked out of the station, we noticed a guy on the corner clapping his
crutches together and yelling, "Y'all motherfuckers are in the wrong place!" We assumed he was just a homeless man ranting to himself. However, we soon realized
we were actually in the dangerous territory of the Surenos gang.To make matters
worse, we were all wearing red, the same color as their rival gang, the Nortenos.
Surenos wore blue, making us easy targets for mistaken identity. We were surprised
by this, as we had always associated gang colors with larger cities like Los Angeles
or Chicago.

The crowd grew until we were surrounded on all sides. Two guys approached El
Nino and Lil Dee, demanding, "What you bang?" El Nino and Lil Dee were confused.
"Huh? What are you talking about? We're not in a gang. We're from Boston." The
guys checked them for tattoos or other signs of being rival gang members. Suddenly,
one of the Surenos punched Lil Dee twice in the head. My dad and I intervened.
"Yo, chill out! We're dancers, not gang members!"

A second later, they lifted El Nino's shirt and one of the guys yelled, "He's wearing a red belt!" Then, he immediately slapped El Nino's head, causing his hat to fall off. Unbeknownst to us, wearing a red belt was one of the most offensive things you could do around Surenos, with people usually getting killed for it in their neighborhood. My dad and I intervened again, saying, "We're not a gang! We're just here from Boston for a dance event, chill y'all!" In the background, women were yelling, "Leave them alone!"

After a few seconds of commotion, they realized from our accent that we were from the East Coast and not a rival gang. We were still in danger, as some Surenos on the block weren't aware of our accent. We retreated one street over, not realizing we were only going deeper into their neighborhood. We arrived at a gas station across the street from the train station, but the gas attendant refused to let us into the store, assuming we were Nortenos. We didn't bother arguing with him and instead ran across the street to a restaurant, but they kicked us out, too.

I was thinking, "Oh my god! These people want us to die!" My dad frantically called his friend, saying, "Yo, you need to hurry up! We're going to get killed over here!" His friend promised to arrive in two minutes, and my dad stayed on the phone with him until he pulled up, tires screeching. We jumped into the van and his friend apologized, saying, "Damn yo! Sorry I didn't warn y'all. Y'all have to be careful out here, especially wearing red in this neighborhood."

All of us were shocked but grateful to be alive because the Surenos were deep! There were five of us and probably around twenty of them. We drove straight to the Cellspace venue in shock, still processing what had just happened to us. I was paranoid the whole time, watching everyone around me. None of us danced that night. Local residents came up to us, saying the same thing: "Are y'all alright?! Y'all are lucky none of y'all got killed! Most people don't make it out alive! Don't ever wear red in that section of the Mission!" After all was said and done that evening, we had to stay the course and complete our mission. We still had to battle and beat some of the best crews in the world the next day.

During the competition, the situation with the Surenos gang took a lot of pressure off us, because we danced as if we were just happy to be alive. We appreciated the opportunity to do what we love and stayed focused on our routines and months of preparation. Although some of us may have had post-traumatic stress disorder, we managed to win the championship. We were the youngest crew competing, and we battled Motion Disorders (Milwaukee, WI) in the first round, Head Hunters Crew (San Jose, CA) in the semifinals, and Massive Monkees (Seattle, WA) in the finals. We gained just about every vote from all five judges for all the battles. This victory was a true testament to life. Whenever things get tough, it's important to maintain your composure and stay focused.

• Flava Squad winning the Out For Fame USA Championship in San Francisco, CA (2006).

Photo: Lonestar

The Big Break

A few months after my crew and I won the Out For Fame national crew title, I received a message on AOL Instant Messenger from Paulskeee inviting me to DJ at the Out For Fame breaking championship in the Bronx. Despite only having a year of DJing experience, I eagerly accepted the offer. My dad was thrilled, as he had been pushing me to become a DJ. I started practicing more when visiting my dad's house on the weekends, determined to prove myself to the world.

I was hyped for the gig, but also nervous. I had never played outside of Boston, let alone in the birthplace of breaking. The New York–Boston rivalry ran deep, and I wasn't sure how I would be received. Nevertheless, I was determined to show what I was made of. The competition was in December 2006, and I spent countless hours practicing and selecting the perfect tracks to play.

When the time came to play at Out For Fame Bronx, I quickly realized the difference between playing for a small community event and playing for a larger, more critical audience. The atmosphere was charged with anticipation, and my nerves were already frayed by the time we arrived at the event. Sadly, I didn't have much experience DJing in general, and I only knew how to play with vinyl at the time. To make matters worse, it was my first gig out of state, and I was entirely out of my comfort zone.

Unfortunately, the soundman had not adequately set up the DJ equipment. Most of the equipment was plugged into a single power strip, which short-circuited midway through the competition, ruining the entire night. One of the turntables repeatedly turned on and off, creating a jarring, unpleasant sound. I could feel my palms sweating and my hands shaking as I struggled to keep the music going.

The judges and dancers looked back at me, and I could tell they were getting frustrated with the music. I hadn't brought many classic breaks or songs to smooth out the vibe on the one working turntable, so I was in big trouble. I went full throttle with doubles of rare breakbeats, thinking I was staying true to myself, but I failed to realize that, as a DJ, there are moments when you need to read the room. We were in the Bronx, and the crowd made sure I knew when I was messing up.

• My first major gig behind the decks. Out For Fame, Bronx, NY (2006).

Despite investing thousands of dollars in records for the event, I was disappointed to encounter technical difficulties when I finally got to play them for the larger crowd. The buildup to the moment had been intense, I had spent months preparing for the opportunity to play for a bigger audience, imagining how blown away they would be by my setlist. But when I looked out into the crowd and saw people scratching their heads, I knew it was a wrap.

At that moment, I felt a mix of frustration and disbelief. I had poured so much time and energy into this, only to see it go down the drain in a matter of minutes. Still, as the set went on, I started to realize that this was actually a valuable learning experience. It taught me that no matter how much you prepare, there are always going to be factors beyond your control. Eventually, we figured out the issue with the short circuit and fixed it. Cros One, the co-organizer of the event, then jumped on to play some funk tunes, bringing the vibe back up.

After the disappointing experience at Out For Fame, I realized that I still had a lot to learn as a DJ. Cros One was initially unhappy with Paulskeee for putting a younger DJ like me on the bill, and my poor performance only worsened the situation. Despite this setback, I remained focused on improving my craft with the help of Paulskeee's advice. In fact, I eventually became the headlining DJ at Cros's Freestyle Session, a prestigious world championship breaking event from 2011 to 2021.

• With Paulskeee at Out For Fame in the Bronx, NY (2006).

Blessings From Hip Hop Architects

NYC has played a pivotal role in my growth as a DJ, teaching me the importance of paying dues in the city that gave birth to Hip Hop. Another pivotal moment in my DJ career came on August 5, 2008. It was the day I played at the iconic Tools of War NYC Park Jam in Harlem's Marcus Garvey Park, the birthplace of the legendary Last Poets. As a serious practitioner of traditional Hip Hop DJing, I knew that playing at Tools of War was a major milestone. The free summer park jam series event brought back the traditional Hip Hop sounds to several parks in NYC and featured elite DJs and Hip Hop royalty from around the world.

The event was organized by Pop Master Fabel and Christie Z., who contacted me after hearing my Latin breaks mix sampler, "That Hard Latin Soul." As one of the few younger DJs representing the traditional DJ Hip Hop form, I was a unique addition to the lineup. People would beg organizers Christie and Fabel to be on the lineup, and even some DJ legends struggled to secure a spot. Tools of War NYC Park Jam was a serious deal, with a huge impact globally every summer.

I remember feeling nervous but excited as I prepared to play classic park jam (funk, soul, rock) breakbeat music from the 1960s, 1970s, and 1980s. The special clause was that we couldn't play any songs with profanity. As I stepped on stage, all eyes were glued to me, but I had the confidence to set off the park jam playing Respect's "Soul Entertainers." The legendary Mean Gene sound system was set up the day I spun. Playing on this classic system in front of veterans added to the pressure, but I was determined to make my mark.

During my set, Pop Master Fabel remarked, "Yo, give it up to Lean Rock, this kid is doing his thing." I played rare breaks and Latin grooves, reminiscent of other Latino Hip Hop DJs like Disco Wiz, Charlie Chase, and Tony Touch. Fabel and the elders appreciated what I brought to the table, as it was something different.

I had gone through a phase of dropping a lot of Latin funk and breaks, which I knew Fabel would appreciate as a proud Puerto Rican. At the time, not many people were hip to old funky latin sounds.

Grandmaster Caz and DJ Jazzy Jay were among the first pioneers to show me a lot of love. Caz, considered one of the greatest MCs who influenced many others, including Jay-Z, Big Daddy Kane, Rakim, and Nas, joked with me, "You can't leave this park with your bag. Give me your laptop and all those records in your bag because you were playing some shit, kid!" Meanwhile, Jazzy Jay, who is also a legendary DJ, a first-generation b-boy, and one of the reasons why Def Jam Records exists, pretended to steal my bag with all my belongings. Seeing their reaction and hearing their response was surreal. They were tripping out because I played rare covers of classic breakbeats they had never heard before, even though they had been in the game since the 1970s.

• Grandmaster Caz, DJ Tony Touch, Kool DJ Red Alert, DJ Jazzy Jay, and Grand Wizard Theodore at Tools of War Park Jam in Harlem, NY (2014).

Photo: Ming Han

I consider myself extremely lucky to have spun at the park jams organized by Tools of War for nearly a decade, from 2008 to 2017. One of the absolute highlights of my time there was building with Grand Wizzard Theodore, the legendary creator of the scratch and the needle drop. After I finished DJing at one of the events, he generously offered to give me a ride to a D.I.T.C. concert at Crotona Park. During the car ride, I couldn't believe my luck when he took me on a tour of the places where Hip Hop history was made: first, the house where he famously invented scratching, located at 168th and Boston Road, and then to 63 Park where he first showcased the technique to the world. It was an unforgettable experience that I think about to this day.

That journey through Hip Hop's roots gave me a new appreciation for the culture and deepened my understanding of what it meant to be a DJ. When I returned to the park jams, I started seeing things differently. Playing there taught me that

DJing is more than just playing rare music. As I watched the pioneers spin classic breakbeats, I realized they were masters at reading the crowd and taking them on a musical journey. They chose records based on the crowd's emotions and could rock the spot better than I could with all my cool, unfamiliar rare records.

These experiences taught me that it's not just about what you play, but also how and when you play it. I was proud to bring something different to the table, but I remained humble and open to learning from the OGs. Breaking blessed me with the mindset to respect and learn from their experience to better my craft. I felt like I had arrived and left my mark on the greats who created the culture that we practice. While my visits in NYC shaped me in many ways, moving to Miami opened up a whole new chapter of growth and discovery.

CHAPTER 6

LIVING THE LIFE: THE P-BOY ERA

· With my mom during my first week in Miami at FIU (2007).

Growing up in Boston, I endured years of freezing cold winters. Moving to Miami in 2007 to attend Florida International University was a dream come true, not just for the warm, sunny climate but also for the unexpected opportunities it brought. One of the biggest surprises at FIU was discovering that we had one of Miami's main breaking practice spots right on campus. It was my chance to build with Miami breaking royalty, Street Masters and Flipside Kings, who had shaped the city's breaking culture.

One person who stood out to me was Lego of Flipside Kings, a veteran of the Miami scene and a revered b-boy legend. Though he may seem reserved at first glance, anyone who knows Lego knows he's a master at talking shit, always in a joking manner, of course. Despite this, I had a great deal of respect for him and his approach to breaking. Lego's style is defined by precision and cleanliness, with a focus on flowing movements executed flawlessly.

During my first week in Miami, El Nino, Lego, and I were invited to battle in Poland as Flava Squad. Back then, promoters would send flight tickets via FedEx to save on costs, but unfortunately, El Nino's ticket got lost in the mail, so he couldn't come. This was a huge disappointment because we had built all our routines around our original squad.

The event we were competing in had a stacked lineup of world-champion crews, including Rivers Crew (South Korea), Def Dogz (France/Netherlands), and Top 9 (Russia). Despite being one of the favorites to win with our full squad, Lego and I were left to battle on our own. We made it through the first round against Ass Kickers from Poland but lost to Top 9 in the second round. Despite both crews hitting us with routines, we fought like we still had a chance. The battle brought Lego and me closer as friends.

Battling with Lego was a unique experience. Most of the breakers I usually danced with were freestyle-based, creating movement on the spot. While I'm not a fan of premeditated sets in breaking, I make an exception for Lego. His attention to detail and precise movements are nothing short of perfection. Dancing with him was a game-changer. He taught me the importance of storytelling, helped me clean up my dance, and showed me how to transition seamlessly from one move to the next.

After months of practicing with Lego, I incorporated some of his techniques into my own style. I learned to control my movements while still allowing myself to be creative and free. Now, my dance is more structured and intentional, yet it retains the wild, energetic quality that drew me to breaking in the first place.

• Lego hitting a freeze in Miami, FL (2011).

Photo: Adam Reign

By the fall of 2007, Miami had become more than just a place to train and go to school. It was a city that defined my new lifestyle. I was wandering through the busy streets of South Beach in Miami with my friends, surrounded by the lively sights and sounds of the city. The skies were clear, and the sun beat down on me as I made my way toward the beach, dressed in nothing but a tank top and shorts. Fancy cars, beautiful women, and loud music filled the air, and the temptation was too much to resist. That's when I saw Wet Willie's, a colorful and lively bar known for its frozen alcoholic drinks.

With my friend's ID in hand, I stepped inside and was immediately hit with the aroma of sweet and fruity drinks. I had never had alcohol in my life, but my friend urged me to try the Ninja Turtle, a frozen concoction that promised to taste like juice. As a longtime fan of the Teenage Mutant Ninja Turtles, I couldn't resist. One sip, and I was hooked. The drink was a perfect blend of sweet and tangy flavors, and I knew I was in for an unforgettable time. Miami was like no other place I'd ever been, and I was all in.

Miami's party scene was wild, especially for an eighteen-year-old like me who managed to sneak into 21+ nightclubs. There were house parties, bars, and clubs every night, and my friends and I were always up for a good time. Even though I was broke, I never had to pay for drinks because my older friends always took care of me. Drinking helped me feel more confident and outgoing, which was great for my social anxiety.

However, I sometimes drank too much and lost sight of my priorities. I showed up to morning classes drunk and hungover, and even missed a few. My partying habits eventually caught up with me, and I failed my first semester as a business management major. I stopped working toward my business degree because I was too afraid to take the required math classes. To cope with my fears, I turned to alcohol as a way to escape.

While struggling with partying and anxiety in college, I found solace in my passion for DJing and breaking. This led me to start traveling to Europe regularly for work. I would finish my college courses for the week and then fly out to another state or country to either DJ for the events or I would compete in breaking competitions. I was always ready for the after-party while on tour. The local promoters and dancers were always generous with their invitations, and I often received free drinks.

Europe was always an adventure, partly because the drinking age is lower than in the U.S., with some places allowing you to legally drink at a bar as young as sixteen. While I loved the thrill of performing and competing, the parties were an unforgettable highlight of my travels. They offered a fun, immersive way to experience the local culture and social scene, and I treasured the friendships and connections I made along the way.

Breaking has always been about more than just the battles; it's about the community, the energy, and the ciphers that form when there's no competition. Few embodied that spirit more than Mex One.

• Mex One at Outbreak in Orlando, FL (2013).

Photo: Daniel Zhu

When I look back on my time in Miami, Mex One's support stands out as a significant factor in my success. I first met Mex after my crew won his Evolution event
in 2007. At the time, he had started his clothing brand Biggest & Baddest and also
created one of the greatest breaking crews of all time, Squadron. He was promoting
his legendary event Outbreak all across the country.

What I loved about Mex was his vision for the breaking community. He wanted
to prove that we could be self-sufficient within our community as long as we did
the work. He aimed to create a self-sustainable economic system within the breaking community, similar to how skaters do in their communities. Rather than solely
relying on outside sources, Mex wanted us to prove we could do it independently
and have more control over the products and ideas we present.

There wasn't anything magical about what he did. It was just hard work. Mex
One grew up as a homeless kid in Mexico and became a successful immigrant business owner in the US. He was just as resilient as anyone could imagine because he
had to overcome the worst to survive. This man was a true visionary, a community
leader, one of the greatest breaking promoters, and living proof that consistent hard
work always prevails.

After meeting Mex at his event, Evolution, in 2007, my friend Dahs took me to his
apartment to pick up some equipment. It was my first time hanging out with Mex,
and we immediately started talking about the NBA season that had just kicked off.
A hardcore Lakers fan, Mex teased me about my Celtics and confidently predicted
that his team would rack up more championships in the years to come. We then
shifted to breaking, debating who the best breakers were at the time. Mex was never
shy about sharing his opinions. Before I left, he gave me some Biggest & Baddest
gear and encouraged me to send him my music.

I began sending Mex mixes and rare songs I had found, and eventually, we collaborated on a project where his designer, Spen, created the cover art for my mix,
Mass Murda Break Mix. Mex was impressed and told me, "Yo Brotha! You may be
the youngest DJ in the game, but you're already one of the illest in the world."

As I got to know him better, I realized we shared a deep passion for pushing breaking to the masses while preserving the cultural essence of Hip Hop. We saw potential in each other, and I became one of his strongest supporters, eventually earning a spot as a resident DJ for his legendary Outbreak event later that year.

Mex's dedication to promoting his brand and enhancing the breaking experience for everyone was legendary. He would drive for hours to attend events, often bringing local b-boys and Squadron members to battle and help run his booth. Despite his success, Mex remained a man of the people, always lending a helping hand even when vending at events. In a breaking community where individual success is often prioritized, his selflessness and dedication stood out as rare qualities.

After two years of working tirelessly on music and supporting Mex's vision, he appointed me as the official DJ for Squadron. At the time, he was looking for new members to represent the crew, as some of the guys were busy with the dance industry in Hollywood. Mex only recruited those with a strong work ethic, a deep love for the culture, and efficiency in execution. Nasty Ray and I became close with Mex and the Squadron during our travels, and it felt natural when he brought us in to help expand his brand. The late 2000s were a golden era for Squadron, driven by Mex's clear vision and relentless work ethic.

In 2010, I embarked on my first European tour with Squadron. We were a crew of b-boys from across the United States, united by our passion for representing our lineages and preserving the essence of breaking on the world's biggest battle stages. Having joined the crew just a year prior, I was thrilled to be part of the experience. Unlike my previous trips to Europe, which were confined to weekend travel due to school obligations, this time I had the opportunity to stay for a full month during the summer.

We traveled from Slovakia for Outbreak Europe to the Czech Republic for SDK (Street Dance Kemp) and finally to the Netherlands for World Breaking Classic to conclude the tour. This was my first time in Eastern Europe, and the experience was eye-opening. Some events were sponsored by alcohol and beer companies, making alcohol more accessible than water. The party culture in these countries was on another level.

At the Outbreak Europe afterparty, one of my friends spent most of his winnings on alcohol, buying over twenty bottles of champagne. He shared some with me, and we had the time of our lives. Inspired by his wild antics, I felt like a rock star when I poured two bottles of vodka into the trophy Squadron won at SDK and made everyone drink from it at the afterparty. I partied hard throughout the three-week tour, drinking every night at jams and events.

These European events had a noticeably different energy. Unlike most U.S. Hip Hop events, which were heavily male-dominated, the ratio between men and women in Europe was much more balanced. I felt this played an essential role in shaping the vibe. Women eased the atmosphere, brought a fun energy, and helped break away from the often macho Hip Hop environment.

I was definitely in awe of this scene. Even though I partied hard, I remained mindful of my boundaries and limits. Growing up with a younger sister, I was always protective of her, and my mom instilled in me a deep respect for women that stayed with me. At the time, I was in a relationship. I wasn't a perfect boyfriend, but it did help me stay in check.

These early European tours reshaped my understanding of what breaking could become. It was during this period that I started to see the potential for breaking competitions to expand beyond their roots in the U.S. Around the same time, the Red Bull BC One All-Stars emerged, and I was fortunate enough to land an endorsement deal with Braun that same year. This signaled to me that breaking was on the verge of significant global growth and evolution.

I often refer to the years between 2004 and 2013 as the golden age of breaking competitions. During this time, doors opened for American crews to travel to Europe and Asia to battle. Before this era, only a handful of U.S. legacy crews such as Rock Steady Crew, 7 Gems, Renegades, Style Elements, Air Force Crew, and Rock Force Crew had the opportunity to tour internationally for performances, competitions, or theater shows. But as breaking competitions gained worldwide traction and visibility, more and more American crews found themselves on the global stage.

As breakers, we may not have been making mainstream rapper money, but we were living a prosperous life, traveling the world and performing for audiences who genuinely loved our craft. It was a dream come true. The global network breaking provided was one of its greatest gifts, allowing us to travel to different countries nearly every week. Few people, even those with financial means, could have experienced the things we did.

At the time, I was simply trying to live in the moment. I wanted to enjoy life, have as much fun as possible, and fully embrace the opportunities breaking had given me. This led me to party more on tour and drink more while performing as a DJ. I didn't know my limits or understand the long-term effects. As I got older and found myself DJing alongside legendary figures in the scene, I started using alcohol as a way to cope with anxiety. It eased my nerves when performing in front of other greats and large crowds.

• Crowd-surfing in Krakow, Poland (2017).
Photo: Dominik Czubak

Learning From Masters

It's wild to think about how I connected with some of the greatest DJs in the industry, especially since I didn't take the typical route of coming up through the club circuit or battle DJing. Instead, I followed the traditional Hip Hop DJing approach, making a name for myself among veteran record diggers from 2007 to 2011 by keeping the spirit of breakbeats alive. I had no idea that this passion would lead to unforgettable experiences and connections with some of the most iconic names in the industry.

Thanks to Forrest Getemgump, I had the privilege of meeting DJ Spinna and Kenny Dope, two legends respected in both the House Music and Hip Hop worlds. As part of the renowned Brooklyn Bandits DJ Crew alongside DJ Scratch and DJ Clark Kent, they were unique in that they had achieved legendary status in multiple genres, unlike most DJs who are known for just one. Their influence inspired me to earn that same kind of respect. Through sharing records and building relationships, I gained their support and admiration. In fact, Spinna even expressed interest in joining my own DJ crew, Horsepower, which was a huge honor.

In the summer of 2007, Spinna gave me my first club gig at Behind the Groove, held at the legendary APT Lounge in Lower Manhattan. At a time when breakbeats weren't a popular club sound, Spinna specifically requested that Gump and I spin rare breaks, bringing back that raw 1970s b-boy energy. As I dropped one of my first records of the night, a disco break, *Bust It* by Craig Snyder, Lovebug Starski (RIP), the man credited with coining the term "Hip Hop," stood to my right. He grabbed the mic and gave a shout-out to Spinna, Gump, and me. I couldn't believe it and thought to myself, "Is this really happening?!" Despite not even being of legal age to be inside the lounge, I played a full hour set of rare breaks. The room was packed with legends: DJ Scratch, Chairman Mao, Ken Swift, and all of 7 Gems. APT wasn't a huge venue, but that night, it felt like the center of the universe.

Between 2009 and 2010, Gump and I became devoted viewers of Scratch Vision, the biggest online platform for Hip Hop DJs at the time. Watching DJ Scratch, a grandmaster and Grammy-winning producer, break down DJ knowledge, technical skills, and business insight was eye-opening. He was intimidating, never giving out easy praise and demanding excellence from anyone who played on his show.

That's why, when Scratch invited me to spin strictly rare breaks on Scratch Vision, I knew I had to bring my A-game. Up to that point, I usually freestyled my DJ sets with minimal practice. But for this, I couldn't afford to slack off. I was still using my dad's turntables, so I had to go to his house and practice relentlessly. I remembered my shaky hands at Out For Fame Bronx in 2006 and wasn't about to let that happen again.

On Wednesday, June 16, 2010, I stepped into DJ Scratch's Brooklyn brownstone, where Scratch Vision was filmed. The walls were lined with platinum plaques from EPMD, Busta Rhymes, and more. As we walked downstairs to his studio, I saw the very setup where legends like Red Alert and Rockin Rob had played. I took a deep breath, knowing I might not impress Scratch fully, but I was determined to leave my mark.

I rocked doubles of every record I had. My scratches weren't perfect, but my breakbeat selection hit hard. I ended the set with *The Howlers - Get Involved*, a rare & unknown cover of James Brown's "Get Into It, Get Involved." As I played it, I saw the online chat room lighting up, with DJs from all over chiming in with admiration. Boston DJs, in particular, went crazy since I was the first from my city and the youngest to rock the show.

After my set, Scratch gave me valuable advice: get better with my left hand on the cuts and keep rocking doubles. It meant the world to me. Scratch wasn't the type to hand out compliments easily, so his words stuck with me.

That moment was a turning point. It gave me confidence and respect in the DJ world. I owe so much to both DJ Scratch and Gump for making it happen. And as Scratch himself would say, "$$$ signs up!"

• Performing at Scratch Vision, DJ Scratch's DJ/Music studio in Brooklyn, NY (2010).

Photo: Forrest Getemgump

By 2010, that confidence was starting to translate into real opportunities. Even though I was still in college, I was booking gigs almost every weekend. It was during this time, while on tour for Outbreak Europe, that I had a moment of realization: DJing could actually be my career. I found myself on an escalator at a mall in Slovakia with Thomas from Battle of the Year and DJ Renegade. Out of the blue, Thomas mentioned that Braun, an electronic appliance company, was in search of a DJ spokesperson for a new campaign, and they needed someone within three weeks. To my surprise, DJ Renegade suggested me for the job, calling me "a young and handsome fella." I was taken aback and unsure of myself, but Thomas and Renegade saw potential in me that I hadn't yet recognized. That moment would change my life forever.

Following that conversation, just three weeks later, Thomas secured the Braun deal for me, and I was flown to Austria for a photoshoot and a commercial for their global "Braun Cruzer Shave Your Style" campaign. The news had me jumping for joy in my house. What made it even more special was that Braun chose to spotlight me, rather than solely focusing on the product in the commercials. My face even appeared on the packaging of the Braun Cruzer 5, which was an incredible honor.

• Braun Cruzer package (2011).

The feeling was surreal when people began sending me photos of my face on products in stores like Target, Walgreens, and other electronics retailers worldwide. It felt like a dream come true, and I was fortunate to do a lot of press for various magazines and online blogs. This opportunity came just five years after I started DJing, and it opened up a world of possibilities for me. With the money I earned from Braun, I decided to invest in my own turntables, allowing me to practice more consistently.

Recognizing my potential for growth, Paulskeee invited me to come to the Bay Area to learn from his network of DJs. Initially, I didn't see the need to delve deeply into the technical aspects of DJing, since my primary focus was on playing for breaking competitions, where advanced turntablism skills weren't a necessity. However, Paul explained that to become a more versatile DJ, I needed to learn more and adapt to different environments.

Paulskeee made me aware that at a certain point, I might not be into DJing strictly for breaking competitions. He encouraged me to look at it from a broader perspective, growing my brand as a DJ to play at clubs, music festivals, and beyond underground breaking events. At the time, I was only 22 years old and couldn't see where he saw me heading, as I originally got into DJing just as a hobby and for breaking. I realized I needed to work on those technical skills as a DJ because my dad also emphasized the importance, much like Paulskeee. Eager to grow, I flew from Boston to San Francisco at my own expense January 7–11, 2011, to connect with Paulskeee and his DJ family, and the first person we linked with was DJ Qbert.

DJ Qbert is not only a master of his craft and a highly respected world champion DJ but also a pioneer in revolutionizing scratching in the DJ world. His approach is both spiritual and scientific, and despite his immense talent, he remains incredibly approachable and kindhearted. When I told Qbert I was eager to learn, he inquired about my equipment. I explained that I had recently acquired turntables but didn't have a mixer, so I had been traveling to the city on weekends to use my dad's setup.

Without hesitation, Qbert walked over to his DJ octagon, unplugged a mixer, and handed it to me. It was one of his Vestax PMC 05-Pro mixers, and receiving it felt like being personally gifted a pair of shoes by Michael Jordan himself. I was in awe and deeply grateful to accept such a generous gift from a true DJ icon. I thought, "Damn, I've got something to prove now." One of the grandmasters of DJing had just given me one of his mixers.

• My first mixer gifted to me by DJ Qbert.

Shortly after arriving, Qbert tested me on his octagon setup, assessing my foundational scratches, drumming, and back spinning skills. I was nervous because this type of structured training was entirely new to me and I felt wack. But I knew it was part of the process. Q quickly recognized that I was at a beginner level and had me practice with a metronome to sharpen my timing. I had never learned DJing with such precision. It felt almost militant. Experiencing this on my first day made me realize, Oh wow, this is way more serious than I expected.

Over the next few days, Paulskeee introduced me to some of the Bay Area's most legendary DJs. DJ Swiftrock taught me how to cut up a song on vinyl using his unique approach to scratching without touching the fader and executing fundamental juggles. DJ Mike Boo broke down blending and scratching across different tempos and rhythms. DJ Deeandroid shared drumming techniques for scratching and introduced me to a Clyde Stubblefield VHS tape, which helped me see the deep connection between drumming and DJing. I practiced beat juggles and cutting breaks in a back-and-forth exchange with DJs Celskiii and Jus Jones. The Bay Area has such a rich history in DJing, and experiencing it firsthand at that stage in my life was invaluable.

Learning from each of these masters was humbling. I believe that in any craft, you have to absorb knowledge from as many greats as possible. That means putting ego aside, even if you have made a name for yourself, because there is always something new to learn. The moment you acknowledge that you do not know everything, your growth accelerates.

When I returned home, I knew I had to take DJing seriously. For the next two years, I dedicated myself to training harder than ever, refining my technical skills and pushing my craft to new levels.

DJing On The Biggest Breaking Stage In the World

After the inspiring trip to the Bay, securing my first endorsement deal, and traveling around the world nearly every weekend, I made a coordinated effort to improve my DJ skills. On November 19, 2011, I finally got the opportunity to play at the largest attended breaking event in the world, Battle of the Year. Spinning at BOTY, the world's first stadium-filled breaking event, was always at the top of my list, which I wrote down in my notebooks during high school. I was inspired by DJ Leacy's sets at BOTY 1999–2001. My mentor Forrest Getemgump had also DJed at BOTY in 2007, and I had helped him find a few tracks for that. I studied all the footage from the semifinals and finals from previous years to see what went well and what went wrong with the music. DJing at BOTY during this era would cement your name in breaking history, so I used that as motivation. I carefully considered how I would approach my first set at BOTY. The most important thing for me was to play at least one set of OG vinyl digs. That was my tribute to the many DJs who had done the same at BOTY, so I knew I had to come correct.

"Coming from the US of A, please give it up for DJ Lean Rock!" MC Trix & MC Spax announced, pumping up the crowd of 14,000 people in Montpellier, France. Instead of cutting up a break as a DJ when they announced my name, I played a signature track and ran onto the main stage to break. I wanted to make a point that, although I was there to DJ, I would always be a b-boy.

A few hours later, I DJed for the first battle of the night between the U.S. and Japan. I kicked off my set with a signature funk and soul groove, setting the foundation before layering in three signature tracks with funky drums and epic horn sections. As the battle intensified, I transitioned into two heavy drum-driven b-boy breaks, followed by a classic breakbeat, before closing with two rare funk-rock records. Everything clicked. The energy felt right, and I could tell the dancers were locked in. I was confident in my selections because I knew this sound aligned with both the American and Japanese styles of breaking, rooted in musicality, rhythm, and tradition.

Though breaking has evolved tremendously since the early seventies, I believe the U.S. and Japan maintain the strongest connection to its traditional foundation, largely due to New York City's cultural influence throughout the eighties. My first set was a nod to that lineage, bridging generations of movement and sound.

With that statement made, I decided to take a different approach for the next battle. My second set leaned more experimental, unpolished yet intentional. I still wanted to capture the essence of a traditional b-boy sound but with a fresh twist. At the time, the French breaking scene was known for embracing diverse musical styles, so I tailored my selections accordingly. Having spent time in Taiwan earlier that year, I was confident their crew would also appreciate the unexpected. I introduced up-tempo Hip Hop instrumentals, blended in a few modern funk edits, and closed with a handful of rare b-boy breaks.

• Headlining at Battle of the Year World Final in Montpellier, France (2018).

Photo: Little Shao

Looking back, the Taiwan vs Japan set wasn't my favorite, but it reflected where the scene was heading. More than anything, I was glad to push boundaries while maintaining balance, keeping the crowd engaged while honoring the culture. Between 2011 and 2019, I had the privilege of spinning at Battle of the Year four times, following in the footsteps of the late, great DJ Leacy. Standing on that stage, I knew this moment was bigger than me. This was legacy. This was destiny.

A Near Death Experience

As my momentum grew, I went on my first Asia tour in 2012 with Abstrak and Mason Rose. Mason Rose is considered one of the greatest videographers in dance and is globally known for his artistic visuals. We had an incredible time partying together in South Korea for the R-16 World Final over the weekend, which was the most extravagant breaking event at the time due to its multimillion-dollar production. I'd never seen that much money poured into breaking culture on a level like South Korea did during the late 2000s era.

We were all excited to spend an extra week together in Shenzhen, China. Abstrak and Mason are some of the funniest people I know, so I knew I was in for a special treat. I'd never been to China before, but unfortunately, we had a rough start. When we landed, we drove from Hong Kong International airport to Shenzhen, China, and went directly to our hotel.

The hotel looked like an abandoned hospital, which immediately made me uneasy. To make matters worse, the street we had to walk through every day reeked of rotten fish. Two days in, while we were roaming the streets of Shenzhen, Mason lost his passport. We rushed around the city to find an Australian consulate only to find out the nearest consulate was three hours away in Guangzhou. There was a specific time window for Mason to get his visa to leave the country, or else he could have been stuck in China for weeks.

Feeling the stress, Abstrak and I supported Mason on his journey to Guangzhou. We arrived the next day, planning to meet local b-boys and visit attractions while Mason went to the consulate. The local b-boys showed us impressive temples around the city, creating a relaxed vibe with fewer people on the streets. With limited midweek activities, we opted to chill, drink beer, and eat vegetarian food, heeding cautionary tales of food-related illness in China.

On the fourth day of the event, guests arrived, and the organizers had planned festivities throughout the day and night. At around 9 p.m., we had a pre-party to attend. Initially hesitant, I decided to go, thinking "screw it" after a stressful week. Luckily, the club was poppin' with massive LED screens, go-go dancers, and unlimited drinks. Mason and I indulged, consuming about two pitchers of Jack & Coke each, turning the night into a hazy, fast-paced time-lapse.

The next day, I was surprised to wake up and find my cousin El Nino in China. Despite my hangover from the night before, I was thrilled to see him, knowing that we always had the best trips together. We joined the event staff for lunch at an outdoor restaurant, but the heat and humidity left me feeling dehydrated. Hoping to refresh myself, I asked for a cup of water with ice. This seemingly harmless decision would soon come back to haunt me.

When I woke up the next day, I knew something was seriously wrong. My stomach was in knots, and I felt too queasy to even leave the hotel room. It wasn't just a hangover from the night before, it was something much worse. The timing couldn't have been worse, as it was the day of the main event, and the promoter had come to my room asking me to DJ.

Despite feeling weak and dizzy, I made my way to the venue, hoping to put on a great set for the breakers of China. But as soon as I arrived, the pain became too intense to bear, and I collapsed on the floor in agony. I left the event within ten minutes and returned to my hotel room, where I spent the rest of the night dealing with the intense discomfort.

I had never experienced such a severe case of stomach illness before. I was stuck in bed, unable to eat, and constantly running to the bathroom. The only thing I could drink was bottled water. After the first day of the event, the promoter came to my room with packages of bottled water and advised me not to seek medical attention in China, warning of the potential risks.

I was angry and frustrated, knowing that I would have to endure this for two more days until I could leave for South Korea, where I hoped to receive better treatment. Unfortunately, my condition only worsened. I couldn't stop using the bathroom, couldn't eat, and felt weaker by the hour. With only a one-day layover in South Korea before heading to Boston, I knew I was in for a grueling journey.

Once I landed in South Korea, my friend b-boy Born picked me up and took me straight to a hospital. When I checked in for my appointment, I was shocked to learn that they were asking for $10,000 for the treatment. I was so sick that I almost gave in, but my insurance didn't cover overseas treatment. Luckily, Born found a much cheaper hospital that could "patch me up" for just a few hundred dollars.

After an hour or so, we arrived at a small, dingy hospital in Seoul. Despite its appearance, this hospital ended up being a lifesaver. The staff gave me a drink that helped soothe my stomach, although I couldn't figure out what was in it since no one spoke English. Unfortunately, I couldn't bring any of the drinks with me for my flight back home, and I only had enough for one day in Seoul.

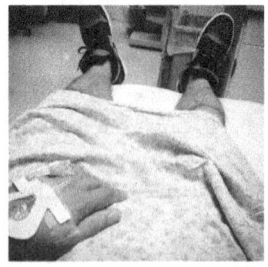

• In the emergency room at Boston Medical Center (July 2012).

The next day, I went on a twenty-hour flight back home. Despite being constantly sick and going to the bathroom every few minutes, I forced myself to sleep until I landed in Boston. As soon as I got off the plane, I called my mom and told her I needed immediate medical attention. My stomach was in excruciating pain, and my body was weak and trembling.

Fortunately, my mom worked at Boston Medical Hospital and was able to get me treated within minutes of my arrival. The nurses immediately put me on IV fluids, and the doctor ran tests that diagnosed me with dysentery, an illness caused by bacteria in contaminated food and water. The medication they gave me didn't work, and I was sick for an additional three days.

I returned to the hospital, where they put me on IV fluids again and gave me stronger medication that finally worked. I had lost so much weight from not being able to eat solid food for a week. The experience left me with severe PTSD from visiting China. The next time I returned to DJ there, I was so paranoid about getting sick again that I slept for four days straight, only waking up to perform at the main event. I didn't shower, wash my face, or even drink tap water. Since then, whenever I travel to an underdeveloped country, I strictly follow food and water safety guidelines to avoid another ordeal.

That experience taught me the importance of preparation not just for travel, but for life in general. I've learned that even the smallest details matter, and one mistake can have serious consequences. That mindset naturally carried over into another major part of my life: organizing.

My Introduction To Organizing

Growing up, I was involved in my dad's Hip Hop events which he had been organizing since the late 1990s. As a kid, I helped him with various tasks like carrying equipment, organizing run-of-show schedules, and putting up posters and flyers. After he gave away $75,000 at United Styles in 2009–2010, my dad wanted to refocus on creating events that were more of a celebration for the breaking community and our crew. During those years, my dad didn't have a strong production team, and with more money involved, there was more stress and pressure. Although it was nice to give away a good amount of money, the main reason he organized these events wasn't for the cash and prizes, but to help the global breaking community grow.

In 2011, I began to take a more hands-on role in event organizing. Despite seeing myself as just a DJ and b-boy, I had been helping my dad with his events for years. So, when we decided to put United Styles on hold that year, I stepped up to help with Mass Appeal and the Floor Lords' 30th Anniversary events. As part of my new responsibilities, I contributed to funding, coordinated talent, created the weekend schedules, and even gave creative direction on the flyer designs.

Working on these events gave me a deeper understanding of event organization and community-building. Around this time, El Nino and I came up with the Mass Appeal concept to unite the dancers in our city. Our goal was to create a competition that was more lighthearted and focused on the element of surprise. The concept was simple: a lottery system that allowed you to potentially switch partners every round until you lost. We were inspired by the World Breaking Classic, but we decided to adapt the concept to better serve our local community. While the World Breaking Classic used the lottery system to create the Great 8 before the Top 16, we utilized it for every battle round to test the dancers' ability to adapt and work together.

We also wanted to give younger dancers the opportunity to battle alongside their idols from out of state. At the time, our community was divided, so it was crucial to us that we create an event that emphasized fun over cutthroat competition. We took the Mass Appeal to Australia and Switzerland in 2013, but it didn't capture the vibe we had envisioned. So, El Nino and I decided to keep the Mass Appeal strictly in Boston, where it was a better fit for the needs of our city.

From the start, I felt that my hometown had a wealth of talented b-boys and b-girls yet lacked the cohesion to truly shine on the national stage. Massachusetts had been a dominant state for breaking on the East Coast, but that success was fleeting and inconsistent. I remembered the two times when we were truly united, at East Coast Overdose 2004 and City vs. City 5 2005 in Illinois, and how we won both events, defeating formidable opponents from Texas and New York. Despite being a smaller state, I knew that if we could build on that unity and consistently work together, we could surpass everyone in the country. It was time to put our differences aside and come together for the greater good of the community. While I was focused on uniting our local scene, a much larger opportunity emerged, one that could amplify our efforts on a national scale.

In 2012, Paulskeee and Cros One approached me with the idea of reviving the Out For Fame USA Breaking Championship. They offered me a leadership role in organizing the entire eight-city tour. At first, I felt overwhelmed, as I was primarily a local organizer, and this tour was for the entire U.S. However, I was honored to take on the position, inspired by the memories of watching Out For Fame 2000 tapes over a decade before. The championship had a significant impact on the growth of the U.S. breaking scene, and I wanted to help push and motivate the next generation of b-boys and b-girls in the country.

At the time, I didn't label myself as an organizer. I was simply having fun with the process. Connecting with people and establishing new relationships in different regions was enjoyable and invaluable for networking purposes. I appreciated the leadership position and experience, as organizing an international or national event can be quite intense. Working with other national organizers called for flexibility and adaptability, as each organizer had their unique approach.

To execute successful and memorable events, it was crucial to have a strong grasp of management and structure, a lesson I learned through organizing the tour. Little did I know, Paul was helping me develop a new skill set in organizing at a national level to add to my résumé. Reflecting on my career, I'm grateful for the time I spent learning from some of the greatest organizers in breaking, who generously shared their wisdom: my dad, Paulskeee, Cros, Mex One, Jo Rawk, MG, MK, Mario, and Tyrone.

Burning Out

While building my career, my personal life faded into the background. Between 2011 and 2013, I was so focused on music and event planning that I had almost no social life. Living with my mom and sister in a small apartment in Stoughton, I rarely left my room except to cook, eat, and shower. My attention was consumed by completing my *Ingredientz of Flava and Free In The Style* mixtapes with DJ B Ryan. During that time, aside from touring as a DJ, assisting the Out For Fame tour, and performing with the Floor Lords, I released a significant amount of material.

But what truly fulfilled me was traveling and playing live at jams. The energy of the crowd, the connection with dancers, and the culture made it all worth it. At one point, I had more gigs in Europe than in the U.S. because European events had larger budgets, allowing me to tour there for longer. In the U.S., I was making $300 to $500 per DJ gig, but in Europe, I could earn anywhere from $700 to $1,000 per gig. Plus, with the Euro being stronger than the U.S. dollar and events having better organization and production value, it was a no-brainer. The only way I could sustain myself as a break DJ was by touring Europe for months at a time.

In 2013, I went on a Euro tour of France, the Czech Republic, Switzerland, and The Netherlands throughout the month of March. The tour went smoothly, and I knew I had done a great job at most of my gigs. Encouraged by its success, I decided to tour Europe for most of the summer, traveling to Slovakia, Switzerland, Spain, and The Netherlands from July until September. The tour started off well, but unfortunately, it took a rough turn.

A week into the tour, The Notorious IBE event in The Netherlands kicked off, and we were all in the courtyard, grooving to the music and enjoying the atmosphere. The vibe was on point, and they were giving away free beer at the event, so I indulged in a few. After getting quite drunk, I tried to dance in a small, heated circle. I jumped into the cipher and began top rocking, then went straight into one of my signature moves. In what felt like slow motion, I tore my MCL. The pain was excruciating and nearly ruined my entire tour.

With seven weeks left on tour and a lot of walking ahead, my injury pushed me to drink and party even harder. I DJed every gig while intoxicated, running on little sleep and often nursing a hangover. Despite having a few friends with me, I lacked the support of my family or crew. Accommodations varied, and I didn't always get to stay in nice hotels. Some nights, I crashed on couches or even floors, yet I was still expected to perform at my best under these challenging conditions.

Six weeks into the tour, I had a gig in Lausanne, Switzerland. One of my friends bailed on the ride to Lausanne, but the promoter reassured me, saying, "No worries, just come the next day." Impatient, I decided to take the train and head there anyway. The event took place at the central station in Lausanne, with the DJ truck only a few feet away. I stashed my bags in the DJ truck, along with my laptop, records, Serato box, and headphones, and then went to grab a beer. As I held my beer, a horrible feeling settled in my gut. Without even sitting down to drink, I hurried back to the truck.

I checked the truck, only to discover that my bag was missing. Someone had stolen it, and I was devastated. Despite searching all around the center, I found nothing. With one more gig left on the tour, I couldn't help but hope to catch the thief and confront them. My laptop was long gone, and I was heartbroken, as much of the music on it was lost forever.

To make matters worse, I hadn't backed up my computer in about a year. After sharing my plight on Facebook, Daniel Zhu of Stance Elements and Jo Rawk of Massive Monkees reached out, offering to set up a fundraiser. Thankfully, within just two days, we raised enough funds to cover the cost of my stolen equipment.

At that point, I was 24, and my life felt like a hot mess. I would go from playing in front of massive crowds in Europe, feeling appreciated, to feeling like a nobody when I returned home. It was a jarring experience to be one of the top DJs in the community and yet struggle to make ends meet. I had sacrificed my well-being for my art.

With social media on the rise and more people having access to you and making comments about your art, it seemed that breakers demanded so much but often took it for granted when it was given. Everything was expected for free, as if I always owed it to the community. Despite these feelings, I knew I needed to toughen up mentally and keep pushing forward. I was tired of feeling underappreciated and not receiving what I knew I deserved. At this point in my life, I realized it was time to leave Boston and level up. Los Angeles was calling my name.

Moving to LA was a turning point. It put me in the right place at the right time, surrounded by people who pushed me to new heights.

• Tokyo, Japan (2013).

Photo: RoxRite

CHAPTER 7

THE STRUGGLE
IS REAL

By 2014, I had become the most sought-after break DJ in the world. After DJing at the biggest breaking competition in the world, the Red Bull BC One World Final in Korea, I had reached my ultimate goal as a break DJ. On the surface, everything seemed perfect, but internally, my spirit was fading. Though my DJ career was peaking, my personal life was spiraling downward.

It was evident that I was using alcohol to cope with the emotional pain. I struggled under the weight of loan payments from my unfinished college education, wasn't making enough money to live, and had my laptop along with most of my music stolen. To make matters worse, I was months behind on an essential Red Bull BC One music project, which involved orchestrating fifty-five brand new songs. On top of all that, I had moved to LA, but just before the move, my girlfriend broke up with me. She had backed out of coming to LA with me, leaving me to face the challenges alone.

I had lived in Boston for most of my life, and although my start in LA wasn't spectacular, I was eager to begin the next chapter. Life felt like it was beating me down, but I knew I had to push forward. Boston didn't offer many opportunities, and I realized that in LA, I wouldn't have to travel as much for work. The city provided more industry jobs, clubs, and events in general.

I needed to learn how to spread my wings and embrace my journey. I had experienced a taste of independence during college in Miami, but this time, I had to support myself without the guidance of my parents or anyone close to me. Even when life seemed to knock me down, I knew I had to keep moving forward. It was a time of self-discovery and growth.

A few months after moving to LA, I started dating someone new, a stoner who introduced me to the city's cannabis culture. With dispensaries on every block, weed was everywhere. At first, it was just part of socializing, but soon, it became a way to silence my thoughts. Getting high gave me a temporary escape, a moment of peace in a city that felt overwhelming.

The more I smoked, the more I leaned into this carefree attitude. At times, I got so high that I couldn't function. I had smoked before moving to LA, but California weed was on another level. It was stronger than anything I had ever tried. Each inhale seemed to lift the weight off my shoulders, even if only for a moment.

At some point, I started wondering what else was out there. Inspired by artists like Jimi Hendrix, who used psychedelics to expand their creativity, I decided to experiment with shrooms. As a music producer, I was curious to see if it would unlock something new in me.

The first time I took shrooms, I sat in my friend's studio, eyes closed, fingers hovering over my beat machine. As I hit the pads, the kick and snare felt like they were pulsating through my soul. Shrooming heightened all my senses, and I had never felt or heard sound clarity at this level before. Goosebumps covered my arms as the music moved through me.

Looking in the mirror, I saw my body stretch like a rubber band, and I burst out laughing for minutes on end. It was a liberating experience, filling me with a sense of adventure and making me feel like a kid again.

The best part? I could create without judgment. The experience unlocked something in me, making me more open-minded in my creative abilities.

• Los Angeles, CA (2019).
Photo: Adam Adolphus

During my experimental stage, I began exploring other genres of music, including Chicago Juke, House, Bass, and Electronic music, and started distancing myself from the Hip Hop crowd. Experimenting with psychedelics while discovering new sounds felt like I was unlocking a new side of my brain, and it was invigorating to experience a fresh start. However, with the newfound creative high came a deep low as I grappled with the worst part of drugs, the comedown.

What started as a means to expand my mind and creative abilities ended up amplifying the real problems I was trying to escape. The stress, loneliness, and gut-wrenching realization that I needed to deal with the reality of getting my life together hit hard. I found myself searching for distractions, anything to keep me from facing what was really going on. Music, parties, and substances became my escape, pulling me deeper into a cycle I wasn't ready to break.

Spiraling

In the spring of 2014, I received an invitation to spin at one of Asia's most popular dance events, Radikal Forze Jam in Singapore. This event was notorious for its wild parties and always had an alcohol sponsor, a rarity in the dance world. At the time, I also had a reputation for being a party animal. I took pride in my drinking, so Radikal Forze Jam seemed like the perfect gig for me.

After an exhausting twenty-plus hour trip from LA to Singapore, I disembarked, and the Radikal Forze team welcomed me with a drink. What started with beer soon escalated to liquor, turning into a sleepless night filled with more drinking at the promoter's house. I didn't even bother checking into my hotel. Jet-lagged but fully awake the next morning, I met up with my cousin El Nino and b-boy Bounce to begin another round of drinks.

I had now gone thirteen hours without sleep. Together, we explored the city, checking out malls in the city center. I hadn't eaten anything, but the humidity and constant sweating kept me alert. The city teemed with dancers from all corners of the globe, and I encountered more of them on every block. As I roamed the streets, fellow dancers offered me drinks, well-aware of my reputation for partying hard.

Twenty hours in, I still hadn't slept and continued drinking. I was scheduled to spin the 7 to Smoke breaking battle, and by that point, I had reached a whole new level of drunkenness. Backstage, I downed a bottle of rum by myself before beginning my DJ set, having the time of my life. Somehow, I remained standing. As the battle commenced, I managed to DJ through most of it with barely any mistakes. The crowd's energy was electric, with everyone hyped by the vibe and music.

Now twenty-two hours without sleep, I kept drinking as I headed to the pre-party. Upon arriving at the pre-party, I had to play a one-hour DJ set. With a bar close to the DJ booth, the drinks never stopped flowing. My drunkenness had reached a belligerent state, and I felt like a ghost floating in the air. Exhausted but determined, I played through my set. After DJing, our driver took me to a friend's hostel instead of my hotel. We continued drinking beers and eating while chatting until sunrise.

I became sloppy and dropped my money and unknowingly lost my passport. I stayed at the hostel, too wasted and tired to care. At some point, I got up to use the restroom but ended up lost in the hostel. Unable to find my way back to the room where my cousin and friends slept, everything went black. Suddenly, I found myself on top of a ladder about ten feet up, only to fall off, landing directly on my right arm. Convinced I had broken it, everything went black again.

When I awoke in another room, my arm was in excruciating pain. It was one of the scariest moments of my life, as I had never felt so vulnerable and lost. I had never before experienced such a loss of control over my actions. Frustrated, I lashed out at the hostel staff, accusing them of drugging me and blaming everyone around me. I was furious with the driver for leaving me at the hostel and was convinced someone had stolen my cash and passport, though they were eventually found in the lobby. I felt set up, and the entire situation was chaotic.

Given Singapore's strict laws, the promoter had to rush to the hostel to defuse the situation quickly. The promoter immediately took me to my hotel, apologizing for not taking me there himself. He told me, "You can take the day off to relax and chill. I want to ensure you can go home with a better experience at our event." He was distressed, his eyes filled with tears. Embarrassed and ashamed, I couldn't recall any of the previous night's events. I spent the day sleeping, waking up only once to eat before returning to sleep.

On the last day of the event, they hosted it at Sentosa, an artificial beach in Singapore. Eager to enjoy my time and have fun again, I grabbed a few free bottles of Jack Daniels they were giving away and resumed drinking. Rather than remaining angry, I just wanted to party and numb my mind. Amidst the festivities, I stage-dove with my injured arm, hosted a twerk contest, and even DJed at some point. Alcohol was my crutch to cope and feel better. The experience of losing consciousness in Singapore had a profound impact on me, and I suffered from severe trauma for months afterward, struggling to understand what had happened to me. But no amount of distraction could erase the lingering trauma. I pushed it aside until life forced me to slow down.

A few months later, in the summer of 2014, I injured my leg while dancing. Injuries from breaking were rare for me, but this one was painful. My girlfriend suggested I try edibles to relieve the pain. I had never consumed edibles before, so she gave me a weed cookie and two weed gummies. Neither of us realized that the dosage was far too high for someone with low tolerance like me, and I wasn't in the best mental state at the time.

As we talked about government conspiracies, artificial intelligence, and religion, the pain in my leg began to subside, and I started to feel good. After about an hour, the edibles hit me hard. Everything we talked about had manifested in my mind into what seemed like a real-life horror movie. It was the first time I had hallucinated to the extent that I felt completely disconnected from reality.

That night marked a turning point. My mental state deteriorated following my first psychotic episode in early July. Believing the edible was solely responsible for my breakdown, I thought smoking from a bong the following week would be fine. Predictably, another psychotic episode happened. Paranoia took over, and I was convinced that the government was after me. Shocked, I tried to sleep it off, but the next day, I was still experiencing the effects of the episode.

• Los Angeles, CA (2019).
Photo: Adam Adolphus

I remained quiet for most of the day, and when my girlfriend asked what was wrong, I just replied, "Nothing." We went to my friend Shiva's house, where the conversation turned to government surveillance of phone conversations. Feeling overwhelmed, I told my girlfriend that we needed to leave immediately. We were already late for our event, a movie premiere, so we rushed to the theater.

To my dismay, the film was about computer hackers, and it opened with a scene of government agencies trying to track down hackers on a mission. That was all I could handle. I had another psychotic episode during the movie, slumping over in my seat, unable to watch. In my head, it felt like someone was playing a cruel trick on me, as if my brain had been hacked. As soon as the movie ended, I bolted out of the theater.

Hospitalized

After the Singapore trip and the psychotic episodes, I faced numerous mental hurdles. I struggled to differentiate between highs and lows and felt indifferent toward life, confused by sudden waves of fear. Despite these challenges, the tour grind had to continue. When I traveled to Houston for an event, paranoia consumed me, making it impossible to find peace in the music and atmosphere. To cope with the overwhelming anxiety, I drank for two days straight.

Once my job for the weekend was done, my friends and I went to a strip club next to the motel to unwind and party. I drank uncontrollably, my mind in pain. Most of the night blurred together, and I stumbled back to my motel room. I woke up the next day still wearing all my clothes and suffering from a terrible hangover. Bedridden, I was unable to get up, ultimately missing the final day of the event. Although I had completed my job, I felt disappointed in myself. It seemed like I was trapped in dangerous territory with no way out. After this experience, I sobered up to regain control of my mind.

Following the Houston trip, I experienced the panic attack on the way to the airport that I evoked in the preface of this book. I knew something was wrong with my mental state, because I had stopped smoking, drinking, and drugs two weeks before. The car ride was so unbearable that, although I was heading to my annual summer European tour, I had my girlfriend turn around and drive me to the hospital. After spending one night there, they transferred me to Del Amo Behavioral Health System for recovery.

During my week stay, I had no access to phones or electronics. My memory of the experience is hazy, as I was on heavy medication for several weeks. Most of it was a blur. The daily routine consisted of taking medication upon waking, participating in group meetings, having lunch, attending more group meetings, and then taking medication right before bed. The food was terrible, and the bed felt like sleeping on steel. I had never been to jail, but I could imagine it had a similar level of comfort. By the end of my stay, I remember feeling at peace and ready to return home.

Missing out on the Euro tour that meant so much to me was a wake-up call. I didn't think I would be able to live normally again. It felt like everything had been taken away from me after that last panic attack. It was time to take care of myself and be more mindful of my life decisions.

My dad came to LA for a week to check in on me. Both of my parents were very supportive during that time. They helped me immensely and made me feel loved. Initially, I thought they would be furious, but they were very empathetic about my situation. I went back to Boston to spend time with my family and ground myself. I spent a month with them, enjoying life without any responsibilities. My family's support and love were instrumental in my recovery process. I attended therapy in Boston for a month, and my anxiety improved slightly.

Returning to LA was tough because I felt embarrassed about going to a behavioral health center. It made me feel like I was crazy. I started seeing a therapist in LA who provided me with tools and guidance on how to improve my mental state through self-care and maintaining physical health. The trauma was so intense that even watching horror movies would trigger me, so I completely stopped watching them altogether.

Thankfully, over time, the psychotic episodes ceased. Although the experience was stressful, it prompted a new life transformation and set me on a path to bettering myself. I realized that alcohol consumption was closely linked to my drug usage, as I tended to experiment with drugs more frequently when I drank. I decided to embrace sobriety completely and get my life back on track.

Addressing Mental Health Awareness In Hip Hop Culture

As I worked on rebuilding my life, I became more aware of the deeper struggles many in the Hip Hop community were facing, especially when it came to mental health. I wasn't alone in my journey. In 2015, Paulskeee and I began focusing on the topic of mental health awareness. Both of us had experienced some rough years, and we wanted to spread our message to the Hip Hop community. Paulskeee had faced significant mental challenges since his father's passing in 2011, and shortly after, b-boy Gerald from his crew also passed away. We were both going through a lot, so we felt compelled to address mental health issues, which are often considered taboo in our culture.

In Hip Hop, discussing mental struggles is often seen as a sign of weakness. The culture is built on battling, bravado, ego, and a warrior mentality. Many of us carry a chip on our shoulders, constantly striving to be the toughest and the best. Sadly, even our elders in the culture struggled with mental health, leaving many without proper guidance. Speaking up requires courage and vulnerability, yet Hip Hop doesn't always create space for those conversations. Paulskeee and I felt responsible for using our platforms to shift perspectives and encourage openness about mental health. It became an essential part of my lifestyle.

As I began to speak out about my struggles, I realized that mental health awareness wasn't just a personal mission. It was a cultural shift. By opening up about my own journey, I felt a responsibility to encourage others to do the same.

Then in August 2015, DJ Swiftrock passed away. I was devastated when I received the news via Facebook. Immediately, I called Paulskeee, Teeko, and Fran Boogie. Swift wasn't just one of the best DJs in the world; he was also a kindhearted man. Though I wasn't extremely close to him, he was a good friend to many of my closest friends. I had the opportunity to connect with Swift directly when I visited the Bay Area in 2011 to study DJing, and I learned a great deal from him during that week. Whenever I spent time with him in the Bay, he exuded a humble and enlightening spirit.

• Learning from DJ Swiftrock in San Francisco, CA (2011).

Photo: Paulskeee

I was shocked when he passed because no one expected it. It hit me pretty hard because I was so immersed in mental health awareness, and I thought that maybe if I had reached out more or been a little more outspoken about what I was going through, it could have helped. It's tough to deal with when you don't get proper closure after someone passes so suddenly and at a young age.

The only closure I got was knowing that maybe I could share my mental health message on my platforms and stay in contact with the people I love. When I've publicly shared the stories of my hardships, people have reached out to thank me. It opened up a space for dialogue to help improve our mental states. This opportunity allowed me to have deeper conversations with people in the global Hip Hop community.

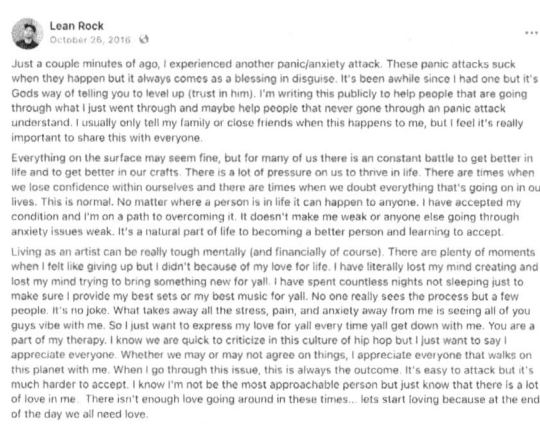

• My Facebook post about mental health challenges (2016).

Let's Talk About It

Two years later, in 2017, Paulskeee organized a mental health awareness discussion panel featuring DJ Celskiii, Fran Boogie, DJ Shortkut, B-boy Kareem, B-boy Jonny U.C., Bas1, Politix, Delrokz, and myself. These were all respected figures in the underground Hip Hop community, and for the first time, we were able to openly address mental health on record at the Mighty4 event in the Bay Area.

Despite the importance of the moment, I doubted myself. I rarely speak on panels, and public speaking has always been a fear of mine. On top of that, I struggled with feeling like an imposter. Was I really qualified to be part of this discussion? I wasn't an expert, just someone who had been through my own battles. But as the panel unfolded, I realized that sharing personal experiences was just as valuable as expertise.

• Celskiii, Shortkut, Franboogie, Jonny U.C., Kareem, Bası, Politix, and Delrokz
at the Mighty4 Mental Health Awareness Panel in Union City, CA (2017).

This panel was significant because it was the first time I had witnessed a discussion focused on mental health awareness in underground Hip Hop culture. It turned out to be an insightful panel, sparking further conversations about mental health. Each participant on the panel was an influencer in their respective crafts. People from rival crews came together to discuss mental health, creating a profound moment for us all.

We all go through hardships, but sometimes we struggle to express them due to vulnerability. It felt like no one was listening to us, so we created our own platform. Other panelists faced similar issues, and they bravely spoke up despite their limited experience with public speaking. Sharing these vulnerable stories was a humanizing experience, especially among so many warriors.

• Mex One (RIP) and his son Beanie at Freestyle Session in Los Angeles, CA (2016).
Photo: Miro Krizan

A few months after the panel, Mex One passed away. I was in the middle of a tour in Switzerland when I found out. As I opened Facebook, I was met with pictures and captions that read, "RIP Mex One." The news hit me hard. I had just seen him in Chicago before leaving for Europe, and he seemed to be in good spirits. I remember him and my dad talking and bonding over what it meant to have a son.

That year, I hadn't spoken to him as much as I had in previous years. At the time, everyone in the Squadron was focused on pursuing their individual goals. We all felt a deep sense of guilt for not being there for one another, and we knew we could have been in touch more often. His passing hurt us deeply, but it also taught us a valuable lesson: to appreciate each other and stay close. That loss reminded us of the importance of connection and pushed us to be more open about our struggles, something often overlooked in our culture. So when Paulskee organized a follow-up panel at Mighty4's 20th anniversary in 2018, I felt a renewed sense of purpose.

This time, I felt more confident in sharing my story. I was not only thrilled to be part of the panel but also proud to participate in an event that tackled these issues to support our community. The discussion featured a diverse range of panelists, including a clinical professional, artists, and organizers. Paulskee played a crucial role in organizing the movement and providing us all with a platform to share our truths.

Despite this progress, I believe the conversation around mental health in Hip Hop is still lacking in many ways. There's so much more work to be done. I hope to continue shedding light on this subject because its significance runs deeper than we often realize as Hip Hop artists. While the panel was an important step in breaking the stigma, my journey didn't stop there. That same summer, I traveled overseas, where once again, music and community took center stage.

• Pia Bordon-Crosby, Gina Mariko, Paulskeee, Freska, East3, Simone Hufana, Anthony Presents, and Delrokz at the Mighty4 Mental Health Awareness Panel in Union City, CA (2018).

CHAPTER 8

MORE LOSS AND REPURPOSE

In August 2018, I traveled to Poland to DJ at the final afterparty of Catch the Flava and to Slovakia for The Legits Blast Festival. These festivals united people from every continent to celebrate Hip Hop freestyle dance and breaking. There was a lot of anticipation for the after-party at Catch the Flava, as the year before, I had hosted Beats and Treats, and everyone was talking about the great vibe from that year. As a result, they brought me back to DJ.

This time, the atmosphere was more intimate. During my set, the party became so wild that I stage-dived into the crowd, an experience I had never encountered at a breaking after-party before. I played nonstop for four hours that night. B-boys Storm, Kid David, Cloud, and many other heavy hitters also attended the festivities.

My godfather Float was teaching workshops at Catch the Flava and judging at The Legits Blast while I was DJing at the events. Anyone who knows Float is aware that he loves to party, too. With all the right ingredients for an amazing party, it was a beautiful sight to see Float, who is twenty to forty years older than most people at the camp, fully embracing the experience. His evident passion for dance was something many people admired and wished to possess.

I was thrilled for everyone who had the opportunity to meet Float, as he is such a special person. He was well-loved by everyone at the camp and ended up dancing the entire night at the after-party. We all had a blast that night, and I was honored to share that moment with my godfather.

• Float at Catch The Flava in Krakow, Poland (2018).

Photo: Dominik Czubak

I hadn't seen Float in a while, so on the bus ride from Poland to Slovakia, we had some time to catch up. He told me it was a lot of work to teach, but he was happy because he hadn't been on a tour like this since the 1980s. I was excited for Float, as he had gone through so much, from going to prison to surviving cancer. He was ecstatic to witness the growth of the global breaking scene and enjoyed sharing this experience with me. I knew this tour would be a defining moment for Float, setting up future opportunities for him to tour, judge, and network.

During the second day of the Legits Blast Festival, I checked on Float while he was judging, as it was blazing hot at the venue. I stepped outside to get some fresh air, and just ten minutes later, Ivan the Urban Action Figure hurried toward me, saying, "Yo, Float just died!" Confused, I thought, "What do you mean?! I was just with him!" I dashed backstage to find everyone in tears.

My heart dropped, and I experienced shock and depersonalization. My anxiety heightened, and time seemed to stand still. When I reached the scene, Float was already in the ambulance, eyes wide open but unresponsive. A staff member from the event rushed me to the hospital. Praying for everything to be okay, I couldn't help but think, "I can't believe this is happening now," as we were in a foreign country, thousands of miles away from home.

When I arrived at the hospital, the doctors spoke little English, making it difficult to understand what was happening. All we knew was that Float was in critical condition. I broke down in tears but did my best to hold myself together. Anxiety washed over me as I made phone calls back home, knowing how devastating this news would be for everyone. Float was the most loved person in my family, and the thought of losing him was unthinkable. It was one of the saddest days of my life.

With him in that state while we were in Slovakia, I had to find the strength to communicate with others and take responsibility for the situation. The only thing I could do was carry his spirit and reassure everyone that things would be okay. I knew that's what he would have wanted.

Due to the brain damage caused by the lack of oxygen when he choked, it was only a matter of time before Float passed. His fiancée, Ivette, and my dad eventually traveled to Slovakia, and we were the only ones by his side before he took his final breath.

Float's passing was an awakening, as I realized the world was missing that positive light. He was full of uplifting energy, offering the strongest encouragement to everyone around him. Despite facing some of the most challenging issues one can endure, he always kept a smile on his face. It was surreal to think about how he had been with me during my birth, and now I was with him during his final moments. I had never experienced anything like this, especially with someone I considered one of my biggest inspirations.

From that moment on, I promised myself to live and appreciate life more. Sometimes, I became so focused on my career that I forgot about the world around me. I stopped being so self-centered and aimed to embody Float and Mex One's spirit by helping others. I ceased placing high expectations on my work and began using my skills in a more selfless way. I wanted to uplift others and make them believe they could achieve their dreams.

For thirteen years, I had always aspired to be the best break DJ, but I eventually realized that this mindset turned into a self-serving rat race. I wanted to do something more meaningful and impactful. Spinning at the Battle of The Year or the Red Bull BC One events was amazing, but after a while, it just became another accolade. While I appreciate all my past accomplishments and will always honor history, it's crucial to continue growing. Float's life instilled a new purpose in me, to live through trauma and still stand strong.

With this shift in perspective, my focus moved from personal success to building experiences that truly resonate with the community. Instead of chasing accolades, I became dedicated to curating spaces where music, movement, and energy come together organically, where breaking culture thrives in its purest form.

• With Janet and Paulskeee at the Mighty4 Float Fundraiser in Berkeley, CA (2018).

Photo: Rob Suguitan

Back To The Essence: Styles No Jokin

Whenever I organize events, my primary focus is on creating a memorable atmosphere through conceptual elements. I carefully curate DJ lineups by selecting DJs who are thought-provoking and bring fresh energy to the dance community. The setting should feel like a sanctuary, with a high-quality sound system delivering clear, soulful music, and the lighting setting the perfect mood. Inviting people who love to dance in the ciphers is essential.

I envision a room full of passionate individuals who adore the music because it sets the tone. My goal is for attendees to feel rejuvenated after my events, just as I felt inspired when I attended Pro-Am 2000 or Rock Steady Anniversary 1997. Both of these events showcased all the Hip Hop elements, with the DJ taking center stage.

This feeling inspired me to start "Styles No Jokin" with my crew, the Squadron. We brought together many of our favorite DJs and created an event that truly embodies Float's energy. The DJ lineup featured legends like Breakbeat Lou of Ultimate Breaks & Beats, DJ Rhettmatic and Mr. Choc of the Beat Junkies, DJ Day, and House Shoes. Our concept was simple yet effective: host a free event in a low-income neighborhood park, featuring talented DJs, music, style writers, and dancers, and welcoming people of all ages, genders, and races.

Bringing such events to these areas is crucial, as residents often have limited access to such experiences. For me, outdoor events are the most enjoyable. Nature is the ultimate venue, and I wanted to recreate the classic New York City park jam vibe. To make this happen, we collaborated with the nonprofit organization J.U.i.C.E. Hip Hop.

• With Breakbeat Lou, Rhettmatic, and Ken Swift at Styles No Jokin in Los Angeles, CA (2019).

Photo: Ervin Arana

The first edition of Styles No Jokin took place on August 3rd, 2019, at Highland Park Recreation Center. This event was particularly memorable for me because the community came together to support and pay homage to Float's passing. During the event, we created a cipher in Float's honor. I played James Brown's "Give It Up or Turnit a Loose" as the song for this tribute.

Ken Swift stepped into the cipher and pointed to the sky, acknowledging Float after he danced on the concrete. Witnessing one G.O.A.T. paying homage to another in such a pure way within a circle of warriors was truly beautiful. Although there weren't many cameras at the event, people talked about it for weeks. It was perhaps the first time in 20 years that veteran b-boys like Kmel, Flea Rock, and Ken Swift all danced together in a circle.

• Ken Swift dedicating his throw down to Float at Styles No Jokin in Los Angeles, CA (2019).

Photo: Adam Adolphus

The energy at Styles No Jokin reminded me of one of the first times I danced with Float in 2006 after he was released from prison. We were at the Strand Theater in Boston, accompanied by my dad, Ivan the Urban Action Figure, and Storm. While Float had significantly influenced Storm and my dad, Ivan and I hadn't yet witnessed his greatness in person. From what we'd heard, Float's skill level was the closest anyone had personally seen to b-boy mastery.

We eagerly awaited the moment he would take the floor. When he finally began warming up, he playfully told us, "Take it easy on me, fellas!" As the music played, he gradually moved from riding the beats on top to executing a quick round of footwork and a fast windmill. Pretending his lower back hurt, he got up, but I knew he was playing around and just warming up to get in his zone.

After a few throwdowns, Float was in his feelings to James Brown's "Give It Up or Turnit a Loose." He started top rocking, performed a front walkover, missed his feet, over-rotated, and went straight into cross-legged halos. We were all so amazed by his performance that we ran out of the building while he was still breaking. As we gathered in the back parking lot, still in shock, Ivan yelled, "All the stories are true!" Float came outside, genuinely puzzled, and asked, "Yo, where did all you guys go?" That was the last round of the day, a true testament to his humility.

• Styles No Jokin 2 in Los Angeles, CA (2019).

Photo: Ervin Arana

After the first Styles No Jokin event we wanted to continue the same energy, so on November 19, 2019, we organized the second edition as part of the Freestyle Session world finals weekend. Knowing that many out-of-towners would be in the area for the Freestyle Session, and that several had asked about Styles No Jokin, we decided to make it happen with the help of Cros 1. Some people crucial to the first edition were out of town, so I focused more on the music to live up to the hype.

I aimed to cover the music aspect from all angles, bringing in DJ veterans Mr. Choc, DJ Day, and House Shoes. They each brought something different to the table and exceeded expectations by playing music not commonly heard at jams. Most of the dancers appreciated the DJs and the art of DJing, creating the perfect atmosphere for the event. The venue we chose, MacArthur Park's Levitt Pavilion, inspired by the iconic last scene of *Wild Style*, was the perfect location, as it contributed to the energy and ambiance that made Styles No Jokin an unforgettable event for everyone involved.

All my interactions with legends and pioneers of Hip Hop culture have given me the mindset and skills to produce valuable experiences as an organizer. Incorporating these legends and pioneers into an event makes it unique, as their wisdom and presence bring a touch of purity. Most breaking event organizers focus solely on the dance competition aspect, often because they are breakers themselves. They may not have experience as a DJ and may not prioritize the DJ lineup. However, DJs and music should be of utmost importance when producing a dance event. When organizing, I focus on every visual and sonic aspect, and I believe that incorporating a personal touch is crucial for creating an environment that encourages the growth and development of our community. As the new year rolled in, I was already thinking ahead, planning the next moves, the next events. But no matter how much vision and preparation go into organizing, some things are simply beyond our control.

The Pandemic

On March 12, 2020, Covid-19 shutdowns began in different cities across the U.S. as I arrived in Las Vegas to do some DJ gigs. The airport was emptier than usual with a few people wearing masks and the TVs loudly playing the news. I thought to myself, "Am I living in an episode of *Black Mirror*"? It was a ghost town. I had never seen Las Vegas airport look so empty. As I walked out of the airport and went straight to the curbside pickup, I looked up to see the sky, which was eerily gray. I told myself, "I hope I don't get stuck here."

The promoter waved me down and picked me up from the airport. While driving, she told me, "It's not looking great for the event. The team may cancel the event tomorrow due to state restrictions, but we'll wait till we get official word from the governor of Nevada." On the way to the hotel, we passed giant billboards with ads making jokes about Covid. I had never witnessed any virus get this much attention, so I knew something was up. I got to the hotel to decompress, shower, eat at a restaurant, and then went straight to the club gig I had the first night.

Everything seemed normal again until I was on the way to the venue. The promoter for the breaking event texted me, "Sorry, but we have to cancel the event tomorrow." Shortly after, I got a text from RoxRite saying, "Yo! You should probably come back home ASAP. It's not looking good. They're saying they are going to lock down LA." I panicked and immediately booked the first flight out to LA. The night played out like a time-lapse. All I could think about was getting home as soon as possible. I was in Vegas for a little over sixteen hours.

I returned to LA, and the eerie skies followed me from Vegas. After all my traveling, I was ready to lay back for a bit. A few hours later, I heard the news that the NBA was officially shutting down due to Covid. I knew it was a wrap because I had never heard of the NBA shutting down for anything but lockouts. I thought the lockdown would be over within a week or two. But boy, was I wrong.

Months went by, and the lockdown was still in effect. We were all still adapting to this new way of living. We tried to figure out what to do during the lockdown as our patience wore thin. Everyone was stuck in their homes for months, living on social media. We all longed to return to our everyday lives, but it wasn't happening. Laws were constantly changing regarding masks in Los Angeles, and the city hadn't enacted vaccine mandates yet. We had limited access to things we could do.

I didn't DJ or dance for months since no gigs were happening and no venues were open in LA. I saw artists turning to online platforms to express themselves creatively, but I wasn't committed to that idea. So, I continued to fall back. In the early stages of the pandemic, it felt like all I could do was eat. Looking back, that period forced me to adapt and rethink my approach to both my work and my connection to the world around me.

Global Uprising

Just as I was beginning to process this new reality, the world shifted again. After witnessing the May 25, 2020, murder of George Floyd, I knew the streets would erupt. People had been confined to their homes for far too long, with minimal funds and little government assistance. Additionally, we were grappling with yet another instance of a Black man being killed by law enforcement. Police brutality has been a persistent issue in America, and with the advent of video technology, it is now being exposed on a much larger scale. This incident garnered even more attention than previous ones, as there were no distractions from sports or entertainment due to the lockdown.

Like many others, I was frustrated and angry about the murder of George Floyd. It was yet another moment of hopelessness and embarrassment for our country, especially for people of color. The eyes of the world were on America, as police brutality and systemic racism have been recurring issues since the nation's inception. Enough was enough.

Five days after George Floyd's untimely death, a protest was scheduled at Pan Pacific Park. The plan was to march down to Beverly Hills. Although I was eager to show my support, a gut feeling warned me that something might go wrong. On top of that, we were still in the middle of a pandemic lockdown. Ultimately, I made the decision to stay home.

Sure enough, as protesters began marching, all hell broke loose. A burning cop car stood at the intersection of Fairfax Avenue and Beverly Boulevard, with a heavy police presence awaiting the protestors. As people grew angrier, the police started shooting rubber bullets and deploying tear gas. Some individuals retaliated by throwing objects, burning cop cars, and fighting back against law enforcement. Others tagged "ACAB" and "Fuck 12" throughout the neighborhood.

Looters seized the opportunity to smash storefronts and steal from businesses in the area. People even fought on the streets over stolen goods. Shops on Melrose Avenue were set ablaze, and by the end of the day, nearly every establishment in my neighborhood had been damaged or destroyed. I was in my house, and it sounded like a war zone outside.

For the next 24 hours, all I heard were sirens and helicopters. In protection mode, I tried to ensure no one would break into my house. I slept with knives beside my bed for a week straight, fearing for my life. Even after my neighborhood had been cleaned up and things had settled down, riots continued in other parts of Los Angeles. It was horrid.

As I watched the news, the president made threats to citizens and sent the National Guard to regulate major cities. They ended up patrolling the streets for days. I had never witnessed anything like this before in America during my lifetime. I hadn't experienced the Civil Rights Movement of the 1960s or lived in LA during the Rodney King riots, I had only seen those events on TV. It was crazy to witness all the tension unfolding just a few blocks away from my home. I felt uneasy, anxious, and paranoid.

Many Black and Brown men in America can relate to having negative experiences with law enforcement. I had my first encounter when I was twelve years old, and I'll never forget it. I had to give a presentation for a drug prevention program in the sixth grade, but when I couldn't bring myself to speak in front of the class, a police officer pulled me out and berated me. He told me, "A few years from now, you'll be one of those kids I'll arrest at a party." Shocked and speechless, I didn't know what to say.

The officer didn't realize that I was just afraid of public speaking. I returned to class with my head down. While he didn't physically harm me, he instilled fear and exerted power over me. It felt like he was picking on me because I was the only Brown kid in class and didn't obey his commands. While writing this book, I researched the officer and discovered he had been involved in multiple police scandals in Stoughton. I guess that speaks volumes about him.

Giving Back

A week after the George Floyd protest, my crew Squadron decided to organize an online fundraiser called Break With A Cause. Kid David took the initiative to make it happen, and I helped direct the project. We created a weeklong Instagram Live campaign to support the Black community, accepting donations through Venmo and Cashapp. Prada-G, Luigi, Keebz, RoxRite, and Nasty Ray taught online breaking workshops during the campaign week, and we brought in the legendary b-boy Kmel to lead the final workshop.

For five days straight, we taught breaking workshops for one to two hours each day. By the end of the week, we had raised over $16,000. We hadn't seen each other in three months due to the lockdown, so working on this fundraiser allowed us to bond while doing something great for the community. Many people in the breaking scene were quick to share opinions on social issues during the pandemic but rarely provided solutions.

Our crew took action by giving back to a community in need. We divided the donations equally among The Loveland Foundation, NAACP Legal Defense and Educational Fund, and Color of Change organizations. This project gave me a renewed sense of purpose after spending so much time at home during the lockdown. From the start of Break With A Cause to the end of 2020, I organized more fundraisers, raising over $18,000 in total.

• The Squadron "Break With A Cause" fundraiser in Los Angeles, CA (2020).

When you're giving back, the energy is positive, and people are motivated to donate to a great cause. I'm proud that we took the initiative to do something bigger than ourselves. It's something Mex One would have been proud of because it represented his values of doing good deeds. To my knowledge, there weren't many, if any, crews fundraising during this time. It would have been great to see even more support within our breaking community.

However, while breaking culture thrives on competition, we often take more than we give. Whether it's community efforts, supporting events, or even recognizing the people who make this scene possible, there's a tendency to overlook what keeps everything running. Nowhere is this more apparent than in the music we dance to. DJs set the tone, create the energy, and keep battles alive, yet their contributions are often undervalued or ignored.

CHAPTER 9

A STATEMENT ON BREAKING MUSIC

In my journey as a breaking DJ, I have come to understand the vital role music plays in shaping the atmosphere and energy of events, while also facing numerous challenges and a lack of recognition for our essential contributions. Behind every battle track is an unseen process, digging for records, clearing rights, producing new beats, and fine-tuning the sound to match the energy of the dancers. DJs do more than just play music; we shape the entire experience, yet our work often goes unnoticed until something goes wrong. These challenges include navigating the impact of music licensing, as well as the ongoing development of breaking music. Through sharing my personal experiences, I aim to shed light on the major obstacles faced by breaking DJs and advocate for increased investment in skilled DJs and original compositions to drive continued growth and innovation in the breaking community.

In 2013, I was hired to DJ at the Red Bull BC One World Final in Korea. I worked closely with Patrick Seddon, the head of Red Bull BC One at the time, who made his best effort to clear music for me to play. Over the past decade, live streaming has emerged as a new phenomenon within the breaking community. To my knowledge, the Red Bull BC One was one of the first events to successfully live stream their breaking competitions.

With live streaming came the challenge of music licensing, as we could no longer play the music we had been dancing to for the past 30+ years. Initially, I planned to play cleared music for the 2013 Red Bull BC One World Final, but I encountered several obstacles in obtaining the necessary permissions. Some of the music labels no longer existed, the publishers were impossible to find, the labels charged astronomical fees for using just a few seconds of a song, or the artists and labels simply refused to clear the music.

Consequently, I had to abandon my original plan and create new breakbeat music. With no time to panic, I had to tap into my resources to produce new music for the event. My good friend B Ryan introduced me to a music producer named Paten Locke, one of his OGs in Little Green Apples. As a native of Boston, Paten and I connected immediately. A record enthusiast and Hip Hop aficionado, Paten excelled in creating dope beats, DJing, and rapping. His understanding of the vibe needed for the event made it easy for us to collaborate and produce music together.

Our goal was to create breaking music specifically tailored for this Red Bull BC One competition. Paten contributed more than half of the tracks to my playlist, and it took 9 months of preparation, countless phone calls, and endless emails to complete the project. We worked tirelessly until the final day of the Red Bull BC One World Final. Due to the time difference, I stayed up for more than 72 hours straight, coordinating with managers, labels, and producers to ensure that I had the perfect playlist.

Together, Paten and I contributed to shaping the future of new breaking music, and this experience had a profound impact on both of our lives. We made a concerted effort to ensure the music stood out during the World Final, as many people had expressed dissatisfaction with the music at other major events. I'm forever grateful to Paten for the opportunities our collaboration brought me and the strong bond we formed. His passing in 2019 deeply affected me, as I had always admired his passion for the entire spectrum of Hip Hop culture.

Although Paten wasn't a b-boy, he understood the importance of music in breaking, not as background noise, but as the foundation of movement. His dedication to creating high-quality tracks reflected what many in the scene often overlook: the music should be treated with the same respect as the dance itself.

• Paten Locke in Berlin, Germany (2009).

It's All About The Music?

A commonly inconsistent statement in the breaking community is that "the music is the most important aspect of the event." While breakers often focus on the judges, the truth is that music should be just as, if not more, important. The quality of music significantly impacts a breaker's performance, and one of the most frequent complaints is the decline in music quality at events. This is often a result of insufficient resources and funding, leading to lower-quality tracks within the scene. With the rise of live streaming over the past decade, the need for original and cleared music has become even more apparent. The records we danced to in the past were created by some of the greatest musicians, while many tracks today are produced at a much lower level.

Despite this, music in breaking event production often takes a backseat. Take, for example, the rulebook for Breaking for Gold USA, which only addresses music length and tempo, setting a range of 90 to 125 beats per minute. However, there's little to no guidance on other key elements, such as the funk, groove, style, drum rhythms, or lyrics that are vital to the event's atmosphere. More context is needed, such as the number of tracks required depending on the DJing duration and the use of licensed music. In many cases, most people don't consider music as crucial to the event's success, but greater education and awareness are needed.

• DJing at the Youth Olympic Games in Buenos Aires, Argentina (2018).

Photo: Micheal Lo

Ironically, DJs often have the heaviest responsibilities at breaking events, yet they receive little recognition or compensation. The focus is usually on the breakers themselves, and while the crowd might ask, "What song is playing?" After a great battle, the DJ rarely gets credit. Most breaking event videos on platforms like YouTube mention the crew or the battle but not the DJ, even in the video captions. This lack of recognition stems from the undervaluing of the work DJs put in. Unlike club gigs, where a DJ might perform for one to four hours, breaking DJs often work for 3 to 12 hours a day over multiple days. For most major breaking events, DJs typically play for several days in a row, often with the same audience. Each day, they're expected to bring a new playlist.

In 2017 at Outbreak Europe, one of the biggest breaking events, I spent 17 hours DJing over three days. This experience led me to track the hours at every event I attended. While I understand that event organizers may not always be aware of the toll this takes, the reality is that finding the right music for breaking is much more challenging than finding club tracks. I've made it my mission to play signature tunes at breaking events, creating my own identity in the process.

Finding the right music for breaking events is like searching for a needle in a haystack. Unlike club music, which is easily accessible through record pools and frequent releases, breaking music requires a much deeper search. I've spent weeks, months, and sometimes years to find or create music that fits the event's energy and vibe. It's a slow and meticulous process, and unfortunately, the financial rewards don't reflect the effort. While top-tier club DJs make multimillion-dollar incomes, the highest-paid break DJs make only $40,000–$50,000 annually, despite the intense labor involved. Not to say the breaking market is nearly as big as the club market, but the work at these breaking events is more demanding and these rates are unsustainable for DJs living in major cities.

To make an income of $50,000 doing gigs on a twelve-month basis, a breaking DJ would need to make $961.54 a week DJing for fifty-two weeks. In the U.S. alone, maybe eight events pay more than $1,000 per event. Setting up tours around the world, having other means of income such as music licensing, and doing club gigs after the breaking events are the only ways you could come close to touching an average U.S. income. Over the years, I've licensed music for events, video games, TV shows, and commercials to stay afloat.

While I've had success in reaching over ten million views on YouTube and accumulating millions of streams across various platforms, these views haven't always translated into the financial returns I had hoped for. My music has appeared in some of the most viewed battles in breaking history, such as the 2017 Issei vs. Willy battle at the Red Bull BC One World Final, which now boasts over forty million views. However, the recognition I've received doesn't always match the hard work and passion I've put into my craft.

Despite inflation over the past two decades, the pay for break DJs has remained largely unchanged. Top-level breaking events still typically pay between $500 and $2,000 per event, and this has remained constant for almost twenty years. Despite my growing accolades and following, I've barely received a raise in pay. Over the years, I've invested heavily in records and devoted thousands of hours to creating and playing music, but the financial return on these efforts has not been sustainable.

Melodies Uniting Souls Inspiring Creativity

Music plays a significant role in legendary events and epic battles. Consider the classic Top 9 vs. Mind 180 battle at Hip Opsession with DJ Billy Brown, DJ Leacy at Pro-Am 1999, Skeme Richards at Circle Kingz 2007, or Cut Nice at The Notorious IBE 2005. We all heavily contributed to making these events memorable with our sound. The best events are remembered not just for the battles but also for their top-tier DJ lineups.

I have DJed at numerous high-level breaking events worldwide, including Outbreak Europe, Freestyle Session, Massive Monkees Day, and The Notorious IBE. DJs play a crucial role in creating the atmosphere through sound, whether it's in the ciphers or historical battles. Music serves as the essence and fuel for breakers to perform at their best. While it may seem like I'm complaining, my passion for music has driven me to continue DJing within the breaking community for nearly two decades.

At this point, there is a pressing need for greater investment in music and DJing. One of the main reasons breaking events struggle to create a vibrant atmosphere is the lack of investment in quality DJs. Opting for a cheaper, inexperienced DJ can ruin an event experience due to poor music selection and inadequate mixing. This situation should be viewed similarly to a bad DJ ruining a couple's wedding musical experience. A lack of investment in DJing within the breaking community has led to many novice DJs playing at most events.

· DJing at Styles No Jokin 2 in Los Angeles, CA (2019).

Photo: Ervin Arana

Unfortunately, the breaking scene can sometimes be toxic due to its rebellious mindset. This environment is often accompanied by mental baggage and a sense of entitlement. When it comes to music, distrust and irrationality sometimes hinder progress within the breaking community. There is a demand for quality music, but minimal support. Most DJs in the community can relate to this struggle, as they often end up with the short end of the stick.

Few people truly understand the amount of work and resources required to prepare for gigs, let alone find or create music. While I've faced criticism for playing similar tracks or had assumptions made about my work, it's important to acknowledge the extensive body of work I've built over the past 15+ years. I've continually introduced new sounds and innovations to the scene. Although I've faced my own challenges, my focus has always been on delivering the best music possible. I believe it's time to not only recognize my efforts but also the work of every break DJ around the world who continues to push the art form forward

CHAPTER 10

A NEW REALIZATION

Despite the obstacles and challenges we face as DJs within the breaking community, I've always been driven by a passion for music and its role in the scene. However, as I continued to navigate these issues, I started to realize that the environment around me was changing. The difficulties of being a DJ were becoming greater, and the impact of the global pandemic on the scene was undeniable. The breaking community had faced so many setbacks, but the industry's transformation was only accelerating.

By March 2021, the pandemic was still ongoing and showed no signs of ending anytime soon. I had just finished organizing the "Supreme Queens" fundraiser for Women's History Month but hadn't done a live DJ gig in over a year. Giving back felt great, but I needed to get back on my feet financially. Every gig I had been doing was either online or at a private location. There was no audience. Most of the venues in Los Angeles were still shut down, and most DJs focused on online streaming.

I knew unemployment was coming to an end in a few months. I struggled personally, thinking about who I was without Hip Hop, as it was what I'd done my whole life. I tried to stabilize my mind, but my confidence was gone. I realized that I might not ever DJ for a living again. Having dedicated over fifteen years to the craft of DJing, it seemed like that chapter of my life was closing. Unprepared for early retirement from DJing, I kept thinking, "I wish I had finished college earlier in my life."

The thought of not DJing on tour anymore was a heartbreaking realization. I missed having people cheer for me while dropping new music or receiving high praise after a DJ set I played. It gave me a sense of purpose. Those small things meant everything to me and motivated me to move forward with the craft, knowing I provided a unique vibe to people.

With those things gone in my life, I realized I needed to work on myself beyond just being someone within Hip Hop. I wondered, who am I as a person? How do I strengthen myself as a person? How do I get more comfortable in my own skin simply existing daily as Lino J. Delgado?

Aside from Hip Hop, basketball played a significant part in my drive as a person. I have always loved the mindset of basketball players and how their philosophy can correlate to the everyday world. I felt I had reached a plateau in terms of my DJ career, so I started rereading basketball self-help books to rewire my brain. I needed to regain motivation in life.

The books that set the tone for me were Kobe Bryant's *Mamba Mentality* and Michael Jordan's *Driven From Within*. I grew up as a huge Jordan fan and a secret Kobe Bryant fan. Being a Kobe fan was a no-no for a Celtics fan, but I couldn't deny his greatness. Paulskeee introduced me to Jordan and Kobe's mental/physical trainer Tim Grover's book *Relentless*, along with coach John Wooden's *Wooden on Leadership*.

I was reinspired by Grover and Wooden's philosophy and could see myself channeling it back into my life in areas that needed improvement. It's all about transferable skills. A few notable things in each book were the idea of giving everything 100 percent effort, sacrificing aspects of your life, having no shortcuts, and paying attention to all the details of the game. Because it's the small details that make the most significant differences.

For instance, John Wooden pointed out that putting on socks incorrectly, which may seem like a small mistake, can cause an injury, such as a blister. This detail can have a domino effect on your performance. He taught the player to be 100 percent prepared for any challenging moment or situation that could disrupt a good performance. I took that inspiration, and now I'm more analytical about how I move through life.

These four books opened up new pathways in my mind, helping me develop a fresh outlook on life. I realized that if I don't continue to DJ later in life, I can at least apply the mindset of hard work and seamlessly transfer the knowledge I've gained to the next chapter of my journey.

Back On The Road

At the end of July 2021, I finally went back on the road for a worldwide tour to DJ. This was the first time I had been in front of a live audience in over a year. After reading all these books and learning more about business to improve my mindset, being on tour felt draining. I felt like a hamster on a wheel. It seemed as though I were outgrowing the mindset of the competitive breaking scene.

While breaking continues to evolve, there is a noticeable gap in pushing boundaries both in terms of education and event production. As I look ahead in my journey, I realized that the scene from city to city wasn't providing the mental challenge or personal growth I was seeking. Too often, the focus is on who won the competition, who's judging, or drama, instead of on how we can advance the culture intellectually and financially. There is a real opportunity here to build a more robust foundation through education and a stronger understanding of basic business principles in the breaking community.

From my perspective, the breaking community is very closed off from society. This creates a lot of doubts within me about a scene that can be mentally toxic. Although I could be doing amazing things as DJ Lean Rock, there are times when I think, "Man, is this even worth it?" There's a strong sense of entitlement among breakers and a lack of care. Most of our events don't run on time because we lack simple organizational standards.

When I talk to people outside of the breaking community about some of our issues, they shake their heads over the things we debate. For instance, many breakers create tension around who came up with a move first. Some breakers will despise another breaker for years, or perhaps never talk it out after they feel another breaker "bit" (stole) their move. These days, it's not unusual for people to create similar movements simultaneously. I'm not condoning biting, but most of our moves are based on what is now the foundation of breaking.

Sometimes, it's difficult to expect someone to be entirely original when it comes to moves. Additionally, it's important to note that there is a significant difference between copying a move and copying an entire style, with the latter being far worse. When debates arise, these issues often stem from individuals not being honest about their sources of inspiration or their lack of knowledge about the dance. In fact, many breakers, including veterans, struggle to articulate the history and evolution of breaking.

It's essential to take pride in one's creative abilities, but no one should come close to a physical confrontation over a move. Most of these problems are easily resolvable, but a breaker's stubbornness and rebellious nature tend to get in the way. We need to emphasize conflict resolution. Agreeing to disagree or engaging in a healthy debate by stating facts are powerful tools that can help us move forward.

There aren't enough educators to guide the next generation of breakers. It doesn't help that divisions exist between our pioneers, elders, and so-called leaders. Some elders tend to pass down toxic qualities where personal gain is valued more than the community itself. If not addressed, this will unfortunately continue to plague the next generation.

Much of this revolves around trying to make a living through breaking or DJing, rather than allowing the arts to nourish our souls. I've learned that attempting to make a living strictly from the scene as a breaking DJ or dancer can be mentally, spiritually, and financially unsustainable, unless you have extremely low rent or bills. Eventually, as you grow older, you come to realize that all the competition victories and gigs can only take you so far in life.

Getting Honored By The Government

However, there comes a moment when the work you've poured into the community comes full circle. In 2021, my crew and I were honored with a proclamation from the Mayor of Boston and a citation from the Governor of Massachusetts. This recognition marked a significant milestone, as it acknowledged our often underappreciated contributions to dance and art. By breaking down barriers, we emphasized the positive aspects of Hip Hop and shared insights on how dance, art, and music could enrich one's life. We were commended for our free community shows, lessons, hosting practices, mentoring individuals worldwide, and consistently doing so for over forty years. We gave back without expecting anything in return, other than respect for our work.

Although some people in Hip Hop may look down on being honored by the government due to its negative reputation within Black and Brown communities, we can't deny that there are still good people within this system. If you're doing great things in your community and not giving them any reason to act against you, it's wonderful to be recognized for your community work. We've tried to find a middle ground, while still shedding light on many issues in our neighborhoods that could have been better addressed by the government. Ultimately, we took the initiative to become leaders and peacemakers within our city. We provided a safe space for the people of Boston and its visitors, going beyond the breaking scene to inspire ordinary folks and teach resilience through breaking to those in our community.

• With my dad and El Nino holding the proclamations in Boston, MA (2021).

While we were honored by the Mayor previously in 2011, we now truly understand the value of such recognition. Only a select number of legacy crews have received such a high honor from local governments in America, including Rock Force Crew, Massive Monkees, Havikoro, and Rock Steady Crew. I have to give thanks to Paulskeee for having the foresight to help us gain acknowledgment from our city and state officials.

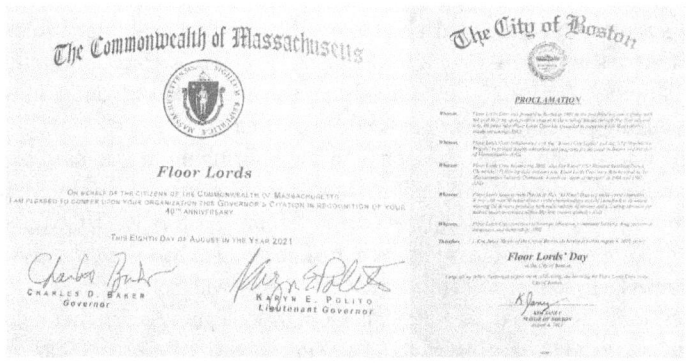

• Proclamations from from the mayor of Boston & governor of Massachusetts (2021).

Always A Student

After the Floor Lords Anniversary, I told Paulskeee I wanted to visit Las Vegas for a few days to seek guidance and determine my priorities and goals. The last time I went to Vegas was right before the pandemic had shut everything down. Interestingly, the same place where the pandemic began for me would also mark the beginning of a new chapter in my life. Upon arriving in Vegas, I was greeted by temperatures well over 100 degrees. Stepping outside was like opening the door to a broiling oven.

Paulskeee picked me up with his mother, Rachel, blasting soul jams as we drove to our hotel in downtown Las Vegas. We passed numerous casinos, clubs, and restaurants, none of which caught my interest. In the hotel room, Paulskeee presented a schedule of everything we needed to accomplish within three days. He had prepared poster boards, markers, and books for our sessions. I had no idea what I was in for, but I came focused and ready to work. It felt like the first day of school.

The schedule included setting short- and long-term goals, something I hadn't done in a long time. Living the pre-pandemic tour hustle, my life revolved around moving from city to city and gig to gig to make a living. When I was younger, I set long-term goals for myself. That being said, between 2014 and 2019, the death of many friends and family members forced me to focus on living in the present. I felt guilty for thinking ahead, which caused anxiety.

My days hadn't been scheduled or structured since college, and working as an independent artist with no security meant that I had to plan my days myself. I didn't have retirement, savings, or many other essentials to life for a long time. The main issue with not planning long-term goals, I learned, was a lack of clarity and purpose in life. While living in the present is important, the pandemic taught me that preparing for the future allows me to prosper during tough times.

Over the course of three days with Paul, I realized that I was my own worst enemy. Paul had a knack for reigniting my self-worth, as I had doubted myself for so long, forgetting who I was, what I had learned, and my contributions to the community. I always considered my knowledge of Hip Hop as common, nothing too special. However, I came to understand that the shared knowledge and wisdom acquired during Paul's lessons were far from ordinary.

Since I was around so many legends in my upbringing, it was hard to look at myself and be confident where I felt my story was important. I always felt like my life was boring, my skill levels weren't up to par, or my story wasn't extraordinary compared to my elders. Paul emphasized the knowledge I had was crucial and powerful because I'd lived underneath a legendary lineage with some of the greatest Hip Hop practitioners ever to do it. I didn't personally look at myself in that light in the past, but I was ready after this building session. I realized everyone has a unique story, and Paul helped me believe my story would inspire.

• Working with Paulskeee in Las Vegas, NV pt 1 (2021).

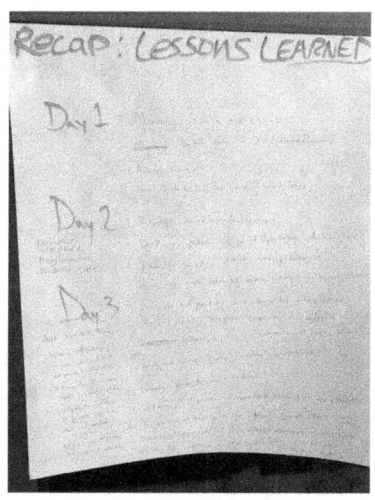

• Working with Paulskeee in Las Vegas, NV pt 2 (2021).

Upon returning home, I gradually began to rediscover my self-worth. My confidence grew in sharing my knowledge to help educate others, and I developed a desire to create innovative projects that could address issues within the breaking scene and Hip Hop culture. Previously a part-time student, I now fully committed to learning in all aspects of life. In the past, I faced obstacles in securing better financial returns for my skills due to insufficient knowledge in negotiating business deals. However, I've learned to ask for help from experienced friends, who provide valuable insights or assist me directly with negotiations, ultimately helping me secure better deals.

I've sought wisdom from individuals outside my circle and successful people in other business fields. Even if someone's career path differs from mine, there's always something to learn and apply to my own craft. I had stagnated, doing the same thing from age sixteen to thirty-two. To achieve my aspirations, I needed to change, break out of my comfort zone, and surround myself with knowledgeable people beyond the breaking circle. This would prevent me from being trapped in the same cycle of daily conversations about breaking.

Recognizing the importance of higher education and diversified knowledge, I believe we should encourage academic excellence within the U.S. breaking community. Although there aren't many high-level Hip Hop practitioners with advanced degrees, most elders in Hip Hop culture express regret for not pursuing higher education or learning more about business. While a collegiate breaking scene exists, it remains largely disconnected from the underground breaking scene, and those pursuing higher education often don't prioritize style mastery or reaching championship levels. Nonetheless, bridging the gap between both sides of the spectrum is crucial for growth to occur. As with most aspects of life, addressing weaknesses is essential to progress.

Recently, someone asked me, "Does it bother you that people call you legends, but most of you don't own a house or have financial stability? In other fields, legends would have more financial stability and multiple properties." This question made me reflect on the fact that breakers must explore various avenues for sustainability, as relying solely on competitive breaking is not enough. Legendary champion breakers may receive impressive social media engagement, but the reality is that views and likes in breaking often don't translate to long-term financial stability, especially as they enter their thirties and forties. Acknowledging this truth is crucial for progress.

My journey of rediscovering my self-worth and seeking wisdom from different sources has led me to a deeper understanding of the breaking scene and the need to address its challenges. Encouraging academic excellence, pursuing a broader range of knowledge, and recognizing the financial struggles faced by breakers and DJs are vital steps toward the growth of the community. As I continue to learn and evolve in all aspects of life, I remain committed to sharing what I've learned, fostering innovation, and making a positive impact on the world of breaking and Hip Hop culture.

EPILOGUE

During the pandemic, Paulskeee called me, hyped, urging me to start writing our own books. He explained that as practitioners, we need to take control of our narrative to break the troubling educational cycle our culture is in. According to him, writing our own books is the way for society to take us seriously as Hip Hop practitioners. While he spoke, I felt a little offended because I had always believed that writing a book was something you did when you finished your career.

In reality, I had insecurities about not having accomplished enough in my life to write a book. At only thirty-one years old, I thought, "Man, I still have a long way to go before I can write a book. Does Skeee think I'm washed up already?" Paulskeee then encouraged me to search for books on breaking and other elements of Hip Hop written by style masters and pioneers. When we looked up the results, we found that there were hardly any books written by practitioners. This realization made me understand the urgency of Paulskeee's call to action. Most of the available books were memoirs by prominent rappers.

In contrast, when we searched for books on sports, martial arts, or hobbies, we found endless titles written by practitioners in those areas. Paul explained that many of the elders in Hip Hop culture, who have firsthand knowledge of its history and evolution, are passing away without documenting their stories and theories in an educated manner. This is a critical issue because it means that master-level breaking and Hip Hop practitioners are not properly controlling their narrative and contributing to the wider discourse about our culture.

I told Skeee, "You know what, you're right. I'll do this book with you, since I don't have anything else going on in my life." I trusted and believed in Paul's idea of publishing because he's always done groundbreaking things in Hip Hop culture and education. The process took over two years and involved so many three-hour Zoom calls and twelve-hour editing sessions. During these calls and sessions, we experienced a range of emotions, including happiness, sadness, exhaustion, excitement, and encouragement.

The journey of creating this book has been amazing. It involved being interviewed, writing, interviewing family, revisiting crucial moments of my life, and collaborating with friends for input. The idea for the book came from the fact that there aren't enough style master practitioners within underground Hip Hop culture who have published their own stories. We believe that publishing is important because it can provide firsthand knowledge and better insight into our culture.

As practitioners of Hip Hop, we often fail to recognize our greatness and the impact we've had on inspiring people around the world. Much of this can be attributed to the lack of financial backing. It's also easy to overlook the legacy we're creating when we're caught up in the demands of daily life. However, our progress is often hindered by the stigma society attaches to our culture. We tend to see ourselves as victims of the system, but it's time to change that narrative.

One issue we face is that we're always waiting for outsiders to document and tell our stories, which can be problematic. They often get things wrong or twist our experiences to fit their narratives. This happened to my father, who had decades of contributions to the city of Boston. Professors would approach him, use his knowledge to boost their own careers, and leave him with the short end of the stick.

We need to take control of our own narratives and document our experiences in an authentic and meaningful way. This starts with engaging in academic spaces to further control the narrative and elevate our culture. If the breaking scene wants to improve our culture and change how the world perceives our art form, we need to take the initiative to evolve in education. There are several high-level practitioners who I know that have paved the way in this regard, including PHASE II, Emile YX?, Paulskeee, Akrobatik, House Magana, Rennie Harris, 9th Wonder, Raphael Xavier, and J. Rawls.

These individuals have either published books, are respected globally for their skills in Hip Hop culture, or have made an impact in academia. Having these practitioners in higher-education spaces changes the conversation, as they bring both authentic knowledge of Hip Hop culture and a high level of academic standing. While there may be other academics involved in Hip Hop education, it can be challenging to listen to their narrative on our art forms if they have never mastered an art or immersed themselves in the culture to learn its history. To move our dance from the underground to aboveground, we must continue to build bridges from all sides. I believe that this dialogue will be key to achieving this goal.

Imagine what could happen if members of the Hip Hop community dedicated time to educating themselves, engaging in open discussions, and sharing information to improve the breaking community's business practices. Unfortunately, I've seen countless talented dancers in the Hollywood industry fall victim to bad business decisions, resulting in wasted potential and financial ruin. It's sad to witness such a tragedy. Additionally, I've observed champion dancers who prioritize their next battle over their long-term financial well-being. These dancers have been around for decades, yet they struggle to see past the next battle because it's all they know.

The reality is, there has never been long-term financial stability in being a breaker or making a living as a break DJ. Therefore, I had to go the extra mile and work overtime just to get the bills paid. However, I have learned that publishing a book can provide numerous opportunities to diversify income streams if you have been performing at a high level in your craft. If you have accomplished something great in your art form, wouldn't you want to have more business opportunities? Writing my book has given me a foundation to materialize these opportunities, and I have only just scratched the surface.

The year 2022 marked a new beginning for me. At my age, I still have a lot of life ahead of me, but sometimes I find myself struggling with old bad habits. Despite this, I am working hard every day to overcome them. One of my biggest battles is with anxiety, but I am facing it head-on, just like I used to battle people in the ciphers. I recently achieved a major milestone by getting my driver's license, something I had been avoiding for the past seventeen years. This was a huge step in conquering my fears and becoming the person I've always wanted to be: unstoppable.

I'm currently pursuing a new career direction, and learning more about mental toughness. I remain committed to guiding others through music and facing life's challenges with the fiery spirit of a b-boy, but also with a more calculated focus as a mature adult. I now see tough times as opportunities for growth and awakening. This is just the beginning of my new journey, and I am excited for what lies ahead. These are the breaks for now.

• Venice, CA (2017).

Photo: Adam Adolphus

MENTAL HEALTH MEMORANDUM ON THESE ARE THE BREAKS!

These Are The Breaks! is primarily an incredible, comprehensive, and as Lean Rock points out, rare history of breaking and other arts, told by a master artist with the unique lens of someone who lived through much of its history and who was deeply connected to the forebears of that history. But the text also holds a hidden gem: It serves as a powerful testament to the healing power of art and community.

As a mental health professional and educator, I was a bit in awe as I read Lean Rock's account of how mental health has impacted his life. While the stigma attached to talking about mental health is decreasing in society overall—slowly but surely—there are many communities for whom sharing about your mental health challenges is still essentially like touching the third rail on a train track—just don't do it. Yet silence around mental health leads to so much suffering.

Lean Rock's courage to share about his own struggles, everything from post-traumatic stress from a serious car accident to coping with panic attacks at the height of his career, is both inspiring and healing. Given those he touches, from the DJing, breaking, Hip Hop artistic communities to the Black and Brown communities he serves through charitable giving, the healing impact of sharing his story is likely to ripple far and wide.

Three threads stood out for me as I read through *These Are The Breaks!*. Lean Rock shares about the importance of developing a better understanding of his family history, and how that history has directly and indirectly impacted the way he had learned to care for his mental well-being. In counseling practice, one of the first activities a counselor will do is to work with a person to trace their "genogram," the history of significant events that shaped their family trajectory. Without labeling it as a genogram, Lean Rock nevertheless delivers a powerful illustration of how the individual struggles of grandparents and parents, as well as the unjust external conditions they had to cope with, such as poverty and racism, all contribute to emotional pain, often unspoken and therefore unresolved across generations.

How do we interrupt the intergenerational cycles of silence around emotional pain, the mental health challenges this pain inevitably creates, and the often unhealthy coping strategies that emerge as a result? Part of the answer to this question leads to the second thread that stood out for me: the power of art to heal. Lean Rock makes this clear throughout the text, and even makes the statement directly that "*Not only was I going to therapy, but I also found therapy through music.*" This insight is as timely as it is ancient, though often forgotten. Today, increasingly, the mental health field is acknowledging that while "talk therapy," aka counseling, is an important and useful component of healing, it is not, by far, the only source of healing. In fact, it is often insufficient on its own.

There is much greater attention in recent years to art as a critical form of healing—one that is rooted in traditions going back centuries. In *These Are The Breaks!*, Lean Rock is able to demonstrate to us how his lifework, which took him from a young breaker in the Floor Lords to his highly successful career as a break DJ, to his ongoing work as an organizer who continues to center music while also giving back to the community, has always been foundational to his healing.

It is common for counselors to ask folks, "What brings you joy?" This question becomes deeply revealing. Most revealing of all is the fact that many people are unable to answer this question. Others can answer it, but in the process of describing their joy, reveal that they have long been disconnected from it and are not sure how to reconnect, or if they can. In many ways, counseling is about helping people find a connection to their joy. There is quite possibly no better way than the arts, in one form or another, to accomplish this.

Lean Rock has spent his life connected to his joy, and at times when he lost that connection, his emotional well-being began to suffer. This raises the third thread that stood out for me: the connection between ultimate mastery of your craft, and the siren song of perfectionism. Perfectionism is often linked to emotional distress. Long-term, perfectionism can impact mental health in the very ways it manifested for Lean Rock: with overwhelming anxiety, including panic attacks. The question becomes, how does a person pursue mastery without the damaging effects of perfectionism? At least part of the answer to that question is the buffering effects of a supportive community.

Most, if not all, humans need community as much for mental well-being as they need it for material survival. We are all interdependent on one another for the things we need to survive—for example, the vast networks that make it possible to go to a grocery store and bring home food, or build homes so that safe and secure shelter is available. And believe it or not, we need a community for our mental wellness just as much. A community can be as small as two people in a household; an extended family; the whole block or neighborhood; or a community of people with like-minded interests, such as the breaking community. However, when it comes to nurturing mental well-being, not just any people will do.

We need healthy relationships founded on trust, love, support, and guidance—and all of that must be abundant, unconditional, and reciprocal. When our communities are unable to provide these key ingredients, our mental well-being will suffer. And when we have access to these kinds of healthy communities but are afraid to reach out to them, for fear of how we might be judged, devalued, or pitied rather than admired, we suffer just as much as if we had no community at all.

Demonstrating the healing power of community is one of the greatest gifts of *These Are The Breaks!*. Lean Rock describes being embedded within a powerful community of teachers—elders and peers—that created the interrelated arts that make up Hip Hop culture, shared and sustained these arts over time, and nurtured the generations of artists that followed, leaving behind an invaluable legacy. Lean Rock also describes the pain that is created when this community at times turns more competitive than collective and when that community stops looking out for one another's greater good.

My hope is that the healing messages incorporated into These Are The Breaks will reach the minds and hearts of those that need it and inspire more people to share their stories, their art, and their collective power to heal.

Dr. Donielle Prince Stanford University Alumna

BREAKING MUSIC TIMELINE

As I embark on this new chapter of my life, I've come to realize the value of giving back to the community that has supported me throughout my career. In reflecting on my journey as a b-boy and DJ, I recognize that my passion for music has always been about more than just creating and performing. It's been about using my talent to make a positive impact and bring people together through the power of music. These experiences inspired me to create a breaking music timeline of classic and secret songs, which I'm now sharing with the next generation of breakbeat DJs.

Breaking has always been an underground thing, and since the early days of Hip Hop, knowledge was often kept secret and passed down only to a select few. This applied not only to dance moves but also to the music that was played during battles and competitions. As a young DJ starting out, I was taught to follow the classic Bronx NYC rules of never sharing music, including song titles and artists. This was partly due to the competitive nature of the breaking scene, but also because the community was relatively smaller back in the mid-2000s. However, as breaking has grown and become more mainstream globally, I've come to realize that withholding this information won't be sufficient for the posterity of breaking.

The following is a breaking musical canon from my perspective based on my research and experience in Hip Hop culture. This is not an end-all-be-all list. This list is based on songs that became popular during specific eras as DJs broke new records. There were plenty of classic rap records that came out during the eras mentioned. But the songs on this list are the ones that had an impact specifically on breaking's inception and global expansion. It's important to note that the musical taste for breaking was different in other regions of the world up until the early 2000s because of limited internet access.

Personally, not every song on this list is a favorite of mine. It's also important to mention the DJs from 2000 up to the present are based on who had a national (U.S.) and global impact in the breaking community based on the major events they played, game-changing mixes, and signature tunes for the breaking scene. By making this timeline accessible to all, I hope to support and uplift the next generation of DJs as they embark on their own journeys. Because at the end of the day, it's not just about being a successful DJ, it's about supporting and uplifting those around you.

1970-1974

This era set the foundation for Hip Hop as DJ Kool Herc extended the break. These breakbeats dominated the NYC community center jams, house parties, block parties, and park jams that would make dancers "go off!". This era of music is composed primarily of Black American artists and embodies the essence of the first-generation Black American Bronx b-boys and b-girls from the early 1970s. Their creation of breaking was based on timing, rhythm, soul, and freestyle ability. Kool Herc set the foundation, Grandmaster Flash came in with the technical perfection, and Afrika Bambaataa had the musical selection to set a precedent for Hip Hop culture sounds. Based on my research, these are the DJs and songs that changed everything.

DJs to study: Kool Herc, Grandmaster Flash, Afrika Bambaataa, Smokey, Disco King Mario, Mean Gene, Kool DJ Dee, Clark Kent, Timmy Tim, The Imperial Jay Cee, and Hollywood.

ARTISTS	SONGS / BREAKS	YEAR
The Mohawks	"The Champ"	(1968)
James Brown	"Give It Up Or Turnit A Loose" "Get Up, Get Into It, Get Involved"	(1969) (1970)
Isley Brothers	"Get Into Something"	(1970)
Wilson Pickett	"Engine Number 9"	(1970)
Booker T. & The M.G.s	"Melting Pot"	(1971)
Baby Huey	"Listen To Me"	(1971)
Dennis Coffey and The Detroit Guitar Band	"Scorpio"	(1971)
Marvin Gaye	"'T' Plays It Cool"	(1972)
Aretha Franklin	"Rock Steady"	(1972)
Manu Dibango	"Soul Makossa"	(1972)
James Brown	"Get On The Good Foot"	(1972)
Jimmy Castor Bunch	"It's Just Begun"	(1972)
Yellow Sunshine	"Yellow Sunshine"	(1973)

ARTISTS	SONGS / BREAKS	YEAR
Hot Wheels	"Badder Than Evil"	(1973)
Incredible Bongo Band	"Apache"	(1973)
Johnny Pate	"Shaft In Africa"	(1973)
Babe Ruth	"The Mexican"	(1973)
Bad Bascomb	"Black Grass"	(1973)
Boobie Knight and the Universal Lady	"Loveomaniacs"	(1974)
The Commodores	"The Assembly Line"	(1974)

1975–1979

In the mid to late 1970s, the disco sound was dominating the music scene, and its influence can be heard in many of the songs that are listed below. During this time, Latino breaking style started to gain prominence and become the format that is still used today. It was also in 1977, after the infamous NYC blackout, that more DJs started to emerge on the scene. This led to the rise of Grandwizzard Theodore, Afrika Islam, and Grandmixer DST, who followed in the footsteps of the original Hip Hop trinity and became the second wave of DJs who specialized in cutting up breakbeats.

DJs to study: Grandwizzard Theodore, Afrika Islam, Grand Mixer DST, Kool DJ AJ, Breakout and Baron, Casanova Fly, Disco Wiz, Tony Tone, Whiz Kid, Disco Twins, Jazzy Jay, Charlie Chase, and Kool DJ Red Alert
(For songs with * the break of the record is played more so than the entire song.)

ARTISTS	SONGS / BREAKS	YEAR
Lonnie Liston Smith & The Cosmic Echoes	"Expansions"	(1975)
Bob James	"Take Me To The Mardi Gras"	(1975)
Dynamic Corvettes	"Funky Music Is The Thing"	(1975)
Blackbyrds	"Rock Creek Park"	(1975)
Roy Ayers Ubiquity	"Brother Green"	(1975)

ARTISTS	SONGS / BREAKS	YEAR
Rhythm Heritage	"Theme From S.W.A.T."	(1975)
Juice	"Catch A Groove"	(1976)
The Whole Darn Family	"Seven Minutes Of Funk"	(1976)
Coke Escovedo	"I Wouldn't Change A Thing"	(1976)
John Davis & The Monster Orchestra	I Can't Stop"	(1976)
Pleasure	"Joyous"	(1977)
King Errisson	"Well, Have A Nice Day"	(1977)
Samba Soul	"Mambo 5"*	(1977)
T-Connection	"Groove To Get Down"	(1977)
Herman Kelley & Life	"Dance To The Drummer's Beat"	(1978)
Captain Sky	"Super Sporm"	(1978)
Chuck Brow & The Soul Searchers	"Bustin' Loose"	(1978)
Rhythm Heritage	"Sky's The Limit" (0:00–0:46)	(1978)
Gaz	"Sing Sing"	(1979)
7th Wonder	"Daisy Lady"	(1979)
Freedom	"Get Up And Dance"	(1979)

1980–1984

Hip Hop continued to spread throughout New York City, eventually going global by 1982. The sound of Hip Hop became increasingly diverse, incorporating influences from various genres. The rise of commercial rap records and the creation of electro-funk music also contributed to this evolution. Additionally, some breaking music even began to incorporate punk influences. As Hip Hop grew in popularity, so did the documentation of breaking and other cultural arts through mainstream media, radio, and film.

DJs and artists to study: Chuck Chillout, Mr. Magic, Marley Marl, Latin Rascals, Jam Master Jay, Cut Creator, and Chill Will & Barry Bee.

ARTISTS	SONGS / BREAKS	YEAR
Spoonie Gee and The Treacherous Three	"Love Rap" "The New Rap Language"	(1980)
ESG	"UFO"	(1981)
Afrika Bambaataa & Soul Sonic Force	"Planet Rock"	(1982)
Planet Patrol	"Play At Your Own Risk"	(1982)
Grandmaster Flash	"The Adventures Of Grand Master Flash On The Wheels Of Steel"	(1982)
Trouble Funk	"Pump Me Up"	(1982)
Orange Krush	"Action"	(1982)
Pieces of a Dream	"Mt. Airy Groove"	(1982)
Man Parrish	"Hip Hop Bee Bop"	(1982)
Fearless Four	"Rockin' It"	(1982)
Afrika Bambaataa & The Jazzy 5	"Jazzy Sensation"	(1982)
Fab 5 Freddy	"Down By Law"	(1983)
Afrika Bambaataa & Soulsonic Force	"Looking For The Perfect Beat"	(1983)
West Street Mob	"Break Dance Electric Boogie"	(1983)
Hashim	"Al Naafiysh (The Soul)"	(1983)
G.L.O.B.E. & Whiz Kid	"Play That Beat Mr. D.J."	(1983)
The Masterdon Committee	"Funkbox Party"	(1983)
Fantastic Five	"Fantastic Freaks At The Dixie"	(1983)

ARTISTS	SONGS / BREAKS	YEAR
Liquid Liquid	"Cavern"	(1983)
Malcolm McLaren	"Hobo Scratch" & "Buffalo Gals"	(1983)
Strafe	"Set It Off"	(1984)
Newcleus	"Jam On It"	(1984)
Davy DMX	"One For The Treble (Fresh)"	(1984)
Rock Master Scott & The Dynamic Three	"Request Line"	(1984)
Grand Mixer DST	"Why Is It Fresh?"	(1984)
Kurtis Blow	"AJ Scratch"	(1984)
Divine Sounds	"Do Or Die Bed Sty"	(1984)
Grandmaster Flash Melle Mel & The Furious Five	"Beatstreet"	(1984)
Ultimate 3 MC's	"What Are We Gonna Do"	(1984)
Run-D.M.C.	"Here We Go" (Live At The Funhouse)	(1984)

1985–1990

Breaking lost some of its popularity in major U.S. cities and certain parts of the world due to overexposure in the media. DJ battles, such as the New Music Seminar and DMC DJ battles, continued to thrive. DJs began incorporating more scratches into their performances, which helped turntablism gain international recognition. Hip Hop music producers also began sampling more classic breakbeats, thanks to the release of the *Ultimate Breaks & Beats* series.

DJs and artists to study: Cash Money, Aladdin, Miz, Scratch, Clark Kent (Brooklyn), Jazzy Jeff, Joe Cooley, Cheese, Premier, Pete Rock, Kid Capri, Egyptian Lover, Steve Dee, Scott La Rock, Spinderella, 45 King, Mantronix, The Bomb Squad, Prince Paul, Dr. Dre and Paul C.

ARTISTS	SONGS / BREAKS	YEAR
T La Rock & Jazzy Jay	"It's Yours"	(1985)
Man Parrish	"Boogie Down Bronx"	(1985)
Boogie Boys	"A Fly Girl"	(1985)
Mantronix	"Fresh Is The Word"	(1985)
LL Cool J	"Rock The Bells"	(1985)
Run-D.M.C.	"Peter Piper"	(1986)
Ultramagnetic MCs	"Ego Trippin"	(1986)
Busy Bee	"Suicide"	(1987)
Eric B & Rakim	"I Ain't No Joke" "I Know You Got Soul"	(1987)
Boogie Down Productions	"South Bronx"	(1987)
Kool G. Rap & D.J. Polo	"Poison"	(1988)
N.W.A	"Straight Outta Compton"	(1988)
Big Daddy Kane	"Set It Off" "Raw"	(1988)
Slick Rick	"Children's Story"	(1988)
Run-D.M.C.	"Beats To The Rhyme"	(1988)
Big Daddy Kane	"Warm It Up, Kane"	(1989)
Gang Starr	"Manifest"	(1989)

The Breaks: *Ultimate Breaks & Beats catalog* (1986)

1990–1995

After a period of decline, breaking slowly began to make a comeback and the culture in its entirety reconnected in the U.S. events such as the Universal Zulu Nation

Anniversary and the Rock Steady Crew Anniversary provided a haven for practitioners of all the elements of Hip Hop culture globally. Knowledge from the pioneers of the culture began to spread, and footage of breaking from the Battle of the Year (Germany) made its way to the U.S. via VHS, creating awareness of the European styles of breaking.

DJs and artists to study: Invisibl Skratch Piklz, The X-Ecutioners (formerly the X-Men), The Beat Junkies, Q-Tip, Large Professor, Tony Touch, The Beatnuts, Da Beatminerz, and Stretch & Bobbito.

ARTISTS	SONGS / BREAKS	YEAR
Hardnoise	"Untitled" (Instrumental)	(1990)
Soho	"Hot Music"	(1990)
Main Source	"Live At The BBQ"	(1991)
A Tribe Called Quest	"Scenario" "Scenario" Remix	(1991)
Black Sheep	"Choice Is Yours"	(1991)
Chubb Rock	"Treat Em Right"	(1991)
De La Soul	"A Roller Skating Jam Named 'Saturdays'"	(1991)
Leaders Of The New School	"Case Of The P.T.A."	(1991)
Eric B & Rakim	"Don't Sweat The Technique" "Know The Ledge"	(1992)
Wu-Tang Clan	"Protect Ya Neck"	(1992)
Das EFX	"They Want EFX"	(1992)
Pete Rock & C.L. Smooth	"The Creator"	(1992)
Redman	"Time 4 Sum Aksion"	(1992)
Showbiz & AG	"Party Groove" "Soul Clap"	(1992)
Ultramagnetic MCs	"Poppa Large"	(1992)
Gang Starr	"Take It Personal"	(1992)

ARTISTS	SONGS / BREAKS	YEAR
Gang Starr ft. Nice & Smooth	"Dwyck"	(1992)
Dr. Dre & Snoop Dogg	"Deep Cover"	(1992)
Lords of The Underground	"Chief Rocka"	(1993)
Black Moon	"Who Got Da Props"	(1993)
KRS-One	"Sound of Da Police"	(1993)
Snoop Dogg	"Pump Pump"	(1993)
Gang Starr	"Code Of The Streets" "Now You're Mine"	(1994)
Original Flavor ft. Jay-Z	"Can I Get Open"	(1994)
Nice & Smooth	"Old To The New"	(1994)

The Breaks: *Ultimate Breaks & Beats catalog* (1986)

1995–2000

In the late 1990s, the commercialization of rap music created a divide as the marketing behind the music didn't align with breaking. As underground Hip Hop cultural events began to focus more on breaking competitions, a deeper selection of breakbeats was needed. At the time, most DJs at Hip Hop cultural events played classic breaks from *Ultimate Breaks & Beats* and 1990s rap records.

DJ Leacy changed the global mindset by emphasizing the need to focus heavily on playing breaking music strictly for breakers. DJ Leacy encouraged a revival of digging for obscure funky records from the 1960s and 1970s to provide the global breaking community with a new selection of breakbeats while referencing the 1970s Hip Hop sound. He headlined at the Battle of the Year World Championship in the late 1990s, setting the standard for premier global breaking competitions of this era.

Underground Hip Hop cultural events with a heavy focus on breaking, such as Radiotron, Pro Am, B-boy Summit, Mighty4, Scribble Jam, and Freestyle Session, also had a significant impact globally through VHS video distribution.

DJs and artists to study: Z-Trip, Fingaz, Static (Denmark), Mirko, Thaid, Honda, Scratch Perverts, Skribble, Leacy, Slynkee, Presyce, Triple Threat DJs, Craze, Eclipse, Charlie Rock, Swift Rock, Derrick Dee, Def Cut, Zeb Roc Ski, Rip One, Pogo, Revolution, Seamstar (Miami), and DV One.

(For songs with * the break of the record is played more so than the entire song.)

ARTISTS	SONGS / BREAKS	YEAR
DJ Shadow	"Organ Donor"	(1996)
KRS-One	"Step Into My World"	(1997)
Lootpack	"WhenImOnDaMic"	(1998)
Gang Starr	"Full Clip"	(1999)
Sway & King Tech	"The Anthem"	(1999)

The Breaks: *Ultimate Breaks & Beats catalog* (1986)

ARTISTS	SONGS / BREAKS	YEAR
Sly & The Family Stone	"Love City"	(1968)
*The Electric Indian	"Rain Dance" (0:00-:45)	(1970)
The Nite Liters	"Nothing"	(1970)
Kool & The Gang	"Rated X"	(1972)
Candido	"Soulwanco"	(1973)
Manu Dibango	"Senga"	(1973)
Black Heat	"Love The Life You Live"	(1974)
Dennis Coffey and Luchi de Jesus	"Theme From Black Belt Jones"	(1974)
Nina Simone	"Funkier Than A Mosquito's Tweeter"	(1974)
*Rare Earth	"I Couldn't Believe What Happened Last Night" (7:10-7:42)	(1975)

ARTISTS	SONGS / BREAKS	YEAR
Bob James	"Farandole"	(1975)
Original Tropicana Steel Band	"Calypso Rock"	(1975)
*L.T.D.	"Love To The World" (3:19)	(1976)
B.T. Express	"Energy Level"	(1976)
The Supremes	"Come Into My Life"	(1976)
Edwin Starr	"I Just Wanna Do My Thing"	(1977)
Rick James	"Fire It Up"	(1979)
A Certain Ratio	"Do The Du"	(1980)
Ray Barreto	"Pastime Paradise"	(1981)
Level 42	"Starchild"	(1981)
James Brown	"Since You've Been Gone"	(1988)

2000–2004

I call this the break DJ era, which saw the rise of DJs who focused mainly on playing at breaking events. Prominent tournaments like Out For Fame, Freestyle Session, Mighty4, and Battle of the Year began touring worldwide and evolved into tournament-style championships. Exhibitions and concept battles such as Who Can Roast the Most and The Notorious IBE became popular.

People began to post song requests and event track listings on various website forums. ed Bull also entered the scene, creating the Red Bull Lords of the Floor and Red Bull BC One. This era was characterized by a dominant focus on competition within the global breaking community, with DJs like Leacy, Woodo, and Ben (aka Billy Brown) leading the way with the European sound.

DJs to study: Leacy, Woodo, Ben aka Billy Brown, Mar, Cut Nice, Tee, Goodka, Siens, Renegade (U.K.), Bles One, Abel, Element, Mista Sweet, Shortee Blitz, Fingaz, Sake & Mane One 1520 Sedgwick DJs (created the first online breaking music show).

(For songs with * the break of the record is played more so than the entire song.)

ARTISTS	SONGS / BREAKS	YEAR
Bernard Purdie	"Soul Drums"	(1967)
Eddie Warner	"Brutus Drums"	(1968)
Mongo Santamaria	"Cloud Nine"	(1969)
Charles Kynard	"It's Too Late" (6:49-7:39)*	(1971)
The Jimmy Castor Bunch	"When"	(1972)
The Soul Searchers	"We The People"	(1972)
Paul Kass	"Causeway"	(1972)
Bobby Womack and J.J. Johnson	"Across 110th Street"	(1972)
Manu Dibango	"The Panther"	(1972)
MFSB	"Family Affair"	(1973)
Can	"Vitamin C"	(1973)
Malo	"Street Man"	(1973)
*Donald Byrd	"Love's So Far Away" (4:49-5:05)	(1973)
Co Real Artists	"What About You (In The World Today)"	(1974)
Barry White	"You Gotta Case"	(1974)
I Gres	"Restless"	(1974)
Sapo	"Been Had"	(1974)
*Roberto Roena	"Que Se Sepa" (0:00-0:42)	(1974)
*Kovács Kati	"Szólj Rám, Ha Hangosan Énekelek" (0:00-0:22)	(1974)
Al Foster Band	"The Night Of The Wolf"	(1975)
Johnny Bristol	"Lusty Lady" Leacy pitched on 45 RPM	(1975)

ARTISTS	SONGS / BREAKS	YEAR
The Futures	"Castles"	(1975)
Jackson 5	"The Life Of The Party"	(1975)
Vern Blair Debate	"Super Funk"	(1975)
War	"Me & Baby Brother"	(1976)
*Henry Mancini	"Theme From Police Woman" (0:00-0:24)	(1976)
*Law	"Wake Up"	(1977)
*Babla	"Aye Mere Dil Kahin Aur Chal" (0:00-0:32)	(1980)
Traks	"Wild Safari"	(1983)
DJ Format	"Lords Of Cardboard"	(1999)
The Herbaliser	"Goldrush"	(1999)
BS 2000	"NY Is Good"	(2001)

2005-2013

After Leacy passed away in 2004, the breaking community faced a significant loss. This created an opportunity for other DJs to step up and continue to progress the music for breaking events. In major breaking competitions such as Mighty4, R-16, Chelles Battle Pro, Circle Kingz, The Notorious IBE, and Outbreak, the spotlight began to shift from just the dancers to the DJs who provided the music. Horsepower DJs, DJs Ben aka Billy Brown, Renegade, and Skeme Richards, among others, emerged as major influencers and innovators in the breaking community, leaving their own unique marks on the evolution of breaking music.

DJs to study: Skeme Richards, Renegade (U.K.), Lean Rock, Ben aka Billy Brown, Woodo, Cleon, Forrest Getemgump, Cut Nice, Nas-D, Kid Skraam, Basic, B Ryan, Cosmic & Arok, Element, DP One, Jus Jones, Light, Wreckx, Rob Life, Mar, Tee, Just 1, Woo-D, Mista Sweet, Ervin Arana, Rockin Rob, Kogataroo, Mr. And-7, Bles One, Dope Shit Productionz, The Bomb Collectors (Nobunaga & Lu-Chiz), and Timber.
(For songs with * the break of the record is played more so than the entire song.)

Hip Hop:

ARTISTS	SONGS / BREAKS	YEAR
Intelligent Hoodlum	"Arrest The President"	(1990)
24K	"We Have No Enemies"	(1990)
Redman	"Da Goodness"	(1998)
Method Man	"Judgement Day"	(1998)
Big Pun	"Twinz"	(1998)
Pharoahe Monch	"Simon Says"	(1999)
M.O.P.	"Ante Up"	(2000)
Royce Da 5'9"	"Boom"	(2001)
Wu-Tang Clan	"Uzi (Pinky Ring)"	(2001)
Mobb Deep	"The Learning"	(2001)
Nas	"Made You Look"	(2002)
The Roots	"Boom" "Web"	(2004)
Nas	"Nasty"	(2012)
DJ Gi Joe	"This Means War"	(2000s)

The Breaks:

ARTISTS	SONGS / BREAKS	YEAR
Sunrise Movement	"Running Wild"	(Late 1960s)
Fred Karlin	"You're Hip Miss Pastorfield"	(1967)
*Crazy Elephant	"Pam" (1:04-1:29)	(1969)

ARTISTS	SONGS / BREAKS	YEAR
Soul Entertainer	"Respect"	(1969)
*Don Randi	"Mrs. Robinson"	(1969)
*Bobby Bryant	"Earth Dance" (2:02-2:14)	(1969)
*Les Flechettes	"Je Vends Du Reve" (0:00-0:24)	-
*3rd Avenue Blues Band	"Come On and Get It"	(1970)
Illustration	"Was It I" (0:00-0:32)	(1970)
The Young Ideas	"I Found Sunshine"	(1970)
*Symphonic Metamorphosis	"Sarabande" (1:34-1:55)	(1970)
Edwin Starr	"Time"	(1970)
The Pace-Setters	"Push On Jesse Jackson"	(1971)
The Terry Cavendish Orchestra	"Leagueliner"	(1973)
Perez Prado and Don Alfio	"Circle"	(1973)
Les Requins	"Campus N° 8"	(1973)
Eruption	"Funky Lover"	(1977)
Cross Bronx Expressway	"Cross Bronx Expressway"	(1974)
Juan Pablo Torres	"Rompe Cocorioco"	(1977)
Choker Campbell Band	"Carioca"	(1977)
Yan Tregger	"The Girl In Gold"	(1979)
The Message & Chris Royal	"Couldn't Get A Name"	(1970s)
Egon	"Six Pack Of Time"	(2003)
Head Automatica	"Brooklyn Is Burning"	(2004)

ARTISTS	SONGS / BREAKS	YEAR
The Budos Band	"Up From The South"	(2005)
Ill Boogs	"Gypsy Rock"	(2005)
The Bamboos	"The Witch"	(2007)
Brownout	"Homenaje"	(2007)
Fusik	"Higher" "Funktana"	(2007)
Jus Jones	"Nitro" "Malanga"	(2007)
Mighty Show Stoppers	"Hippy Skippy Moon Strut"	(2007)
The Apples	"Killing"	(2007)
Funky Bijou	"Funky Bijou Anthem"	(2010)
DJ Pump	"Game Theory"	(2011)
Peace of Mind	"ITL"	(2011)
Funky Bijou	"Aie Caramba"	(2012)

2014–2020

Red Bull BC One, Battle Of The Year, Freestyle Session, and Silverback events have dominated the influence in the breaking community. With more events being live streamed, there was a growing demand for original music specifically produced for breaking. Prior to this time, Mr. Wiggles, DJ Format, Zeb Roc Ski, Z-Trip, DJ Junk, DJ Tee, Funky Bijou, Bles One, and others had already produced music for breaking. However, I saw an opportunity to further develop a playlist inspired by the *Ultimate Breaks & Beats* sound, and this movement grew organically. In 2014, I helped pioneer this new approach by contributing original music, and DJ Fleg and Nobunaga also made their own impact by following suit.

DJs to study: Fleg, Nobunaga, Bles One, Skeme Richards, Ervin Arana, Plash, Smirnoff, South Scream, One Up, Uragun, Marrrtin, Koco aka Shimokita, B Ryan, Mar, Tee, Help, Timber and Lean Rock.

(For songs with *, the break of the record is played more so than the entire song.)

ARTISTS	SONGS / BREAKS	YEAR
*Booker T. Averheart	"Heart 'N Soul" (0:57–1:21)	(1970s)
Slim Thug	"Playa You Don't Know" (Instrumental) Nobunaga pitches the record up	(2005)
Bles One	"TheM Team Theme"	(2007)
Mophono	"The Edge" (Skip on Beat Remix)	(2008)
DJ Fleg	"Otis"	(2012)
Talib Kweli	"Let Em In" (Instrumental) Pitched to 110 BPM	(2012)
Pete Cannon	"YoOoOoOo" Pitched to 118 BPM	(2013)
Rusya Jam Crew	"Up Your Skillz" Nobunaga pitches the record up	(2013)
DJ Bles One	"Happy House"	(2013)
Smuff	"Dawn" Pitched to 102 BPM	(2014)
King P Pete	"The Zip" Pitched to 114 BPM	(2014)
Lean Rock & B. Bravo	"Rambo"	(2014)
Lean Rock & Starship Connection	"Steam Engine"	(2014)
DJ Fleg	"Chelles"	(2014)
XXTRAKT	"Higher" (Massappeals HAF Remix) Edit by Nobunaga	(2014)
D.R.U.G.S. Beats	"Two" Pitched to 102 BPM	(2015)
DJ Fleg	"Clive's Chords" "New Horns" "Cali"	(2015)
DJ Bles One	"Bombshell Remix"	(2015)
DJ Fleg	"Akira" "Obie Trice"	(2016)
Lean Rock & B. Bravo	"Red Light" "Ghost Pepper"	(2017)

ARTISTS	SONGS / BREAKS	YEAR
DJ Fleg	"Granada"	(2017)
DJ Bles One	"Don't Cry Over Broken Bones"	(2017)
Lean Rock & B. Bravo	"Samurai" "Shadowboxing"	(2018)
DJ Fleg	"Catch Wreck"	(2018)
Nobunaga	"Zapp!"	(2018)
DJ Fleg	"Gospel of Fleg" "Indian Burn (Sei Do Sei)"	(2019)

Breakbeat Mix Inspiration

The five mixes that greatly influenced my approach and taste in breakbeats and breakbeat mixes are Mr. Wiggles' *Rock Steady Break Beats* Vol 1, DJ Leacy's *B-boy and B-girl Funk*, DJ Timber's *Live from the Timberdrome*, DJ Forrest Getemgump's *The Best Part* Vol 1, and the P Brothers' *The Zulu Beat*. Whenever I create a mix, I revisit these influential mixes to ensure I capture the essence and feeling they embody. These mixes hold a special place in my heart as they were in heavy rotation during my early years of breaking at the Floor Lords' old practice spot, Hennigan Elementary School. In fact, we even used a portion of DJ Leacy's *B-boy and B-girl Funk* mix for the Floor Lords' performances in the late 1990s.

Mr. Wiggles and DJ Leacy mixes, which were production-based, employed a cut and layered approach, reminiscent of the Latin Rascals, Double Dee & Steinski, and Mantronix megamixes of the 1980s. These mixes featured funky and soulful songs layered over hard drum breaks. Though I generally don't prefer breakbeat remixes of songs, the Mr. Wiggles and Leacy mixes perfected this style. Their tastefulness stems from the musical selection, sample choices, arrangement of music, and innovation of the time.

The production on the mixes humanized them, as the drums were not quantized. The sample selection was raw, funky, and soulful, and both mixes were high-energy. If you listen closely, you can still hear songs that people have not discovered today. Both mixes struck the perfect balance between breakbeat classics and unknown gems.

Forrest Getemgump's *The Best Part* Vol. 1 is similar to the Mr. Wiggles and DJ Leacy mix but slightly rawer. The breaks are cut similarly, but Gump's mix is not layered. Listening to Gump's mix transports me back to classic Saturday nights at Brooklyn Sole, where the lights were dim and people were getting down, ciphering.

Gump premiered many of the beats on that mix at Brooklyn Sole, and it inspired me through its selection of heavy drum breaks. Several of these breaks would become future classics in the breaking scene after 2005.

Around the time *The Best Part* mix was released, Gump kept mentioning the P Brothers (U.K.) as some of the best in the business regarding breakbeats. I finally heard *The Zulu Beat* mix three years after its release, and it was a tribute to Afrika Islam of the Zulu Nation's WHBI radio show *Zulu Beats*, one of the first Hip Hop radio shows. The mix featured forgotten classic rap singles, electro tunes, and one of the hardest breakbeat sections ever. It was mind-blowing because they had used four records that I had wanted to use on my mix, three years before I actually did. I took great pride in having breaks that people had never heard, but these guys were clearly ahead of me. The mix contained some of the hardest breakbeats I had ever heard, and it took me years to find most of the tracklist, which was unusual for me.

One of my favorite statements the P Brothers made to Gump was, "Clean the record store of all its drums." This motto resonated with me for years, and it's easy to see why the P Brothers were light-years ahead of the game. Their authenticity and consistency in digging and cutting up breakbeats since 1986 is why they played so much heat that many of us hadn't heard before.

DJ Timber's *Live from the Timberdrome* has been a personal favorite for years. This raw mix gives the impression that Timber was playing live at a jam. While I appreciate a mix that seems meticulously crafted, I also value one that appears to have been created in a single shot. This mix captures the essence of a live DJ set, striking the perfect balance between classic breaks, rare heavy breakbeats, and captivating funk grooves. I admire its lack of overproduction, as it remains raw, simple, and to the point. In the summer of 2007, this mix was in heavy rotation at the Floor Lords' practices.

My Process Of Making A Mix

Creating a mix is a time-consuming process. It can take hours, days, months, or even years to find the right music that fits the vibe I'm going for, which is why I don't release them frequently. I have high standards and a distinct taste in music, and each mix serves a specific purpose, often addressing something I feel is missing from the breaking scene at the time. There are many ways to approach a mix – whether it's based on a theme, genre, a live set, or a production-based recording.

Most of my mixes have a live feel, and I intentionally avoid overproducing them. I believe it's crucial for a live performance to sound just as good, if not better, than a recorded mix. Early in my DJ career, I even left minor mistakes in my mixes to keep that human touch. It wasn't until about a decade later that I adopted a more perfectionist approach. Another key element in my mixes is introducing new, unheard music, offering fresh inspiration to my listeners. I also incorporate scratches and manual loops to add a distinct Hip Hop flavor.

When it comes to blending songs, I aim for clean transitions by selecting parts of tracks with minimal instrumentation. Using Serato, I set cue points at specific parts of the track. I try to avoid blending vocals over vocals, as it can create a chaotic sound. To ensure a smooth blend, I carefully manage the volume faders and use high/low pass filters, adjusting the highs, mids, and lows as needed. Occasionally, I'll add echo effects or reverb during complex transitions, but I always recommend avoiding effects when first learning to DJ.

The following sections will delve into the specific creative process behind some of the mixes I've made: *We Funk x Lean Rock, Free In The Style Vol. 2, Live @ Styles No Jokin*, and *Now Serving*.

• Mix cover by Kenski (2014).

We Funk x Lean Rock - Show 763 - January 10, 2014

In the summer of 2013, I was touring Europe when I ran into DJ Static from Canada at Bar Stall 6 in Zurich, Switzerland. After his DJ set, he approached me and said, "Yo man, it's dope to see you out here. How long are you around for?" I told him I was on tour for another month, and he followed up with, "Well, when you get home, let me know when you're down to make a mix for We Funk Radio. It's long overdue!" I was excited and quickly agreed, saying, "Hell yeah, it is!"

I've been a fan of DJ Static and Professor Groove's legendary show since the early 2000s, so it was an honor to be the first break DJ outside of Canada to have the chance to make a mix for them. We Funk Radio has been delivering quality funk, soul, and Hip Hop internet radio shows since 1996, with more than 1,000 episodes to date. I studied their past mixes to understand the vibe I needed, aiming to capture the funk and Hip Hop sound they're known for while showcasing my personal taste. I designed the mix with six different vibes in mind.

I started the mix at 103 BPM and gradually increased the tempo to 118 BPM. The first section featured newer Hip Hop instrumentals, followed by classic rap, more recent rap from that period, funk and soul, breaks and new funk, and finally, beats produced by Paten Locke and myself. I wanted to take listeners on a journey, with each song flowing into the next through wordplay, original samples, and vibe. For example, I transitioned from the rap section to the funk and soul section by blending Oh No's "Move" into the Freqnik & WDRE edit of The Rimshots' "Dance Girl." The "Move" track samples the "Dance Girl" drums, which made the genre shift and transition seamless.

One of my main inspirations for this mix was a legendary DJ set by DJ Riz of Crooklyn Clan at a party at the Good Life (Boston) in the late 2000s. He played original samples of rap songs alongside the actual rap tracks, educating and entertaining us through his impeccable mixing. That set still stands out as one of the best I've ever heard.

I also have to credit my good friend DJ Shame and his Traveling Through Sampleland mix from 1993 for inspiring a whole generation of DJs and producers, including myself. At the time, no one was using original samples in up-tempo breakbeat mixes or live at breaking events, so I started doing it. It became my way of providing an educational experience for the audience while paying tribute to the original artists and highlighting music history.

There was some wordplay mixing in the We Funk mix as well. I transitioned from Mac Miller's "Bird Call" to Mobb Deep's "The Learning (Burn)". In the 47-second mark of "Bird Call," Mac Miller repetitively says "Burn One," which aligns perfectly with the chorus of "The Learning." It wasn't the most complex transition, but it was a clever use of wordplay that worked well.

Wordplay/phrase mixing is a popular technique in the DJ world. DJ Dummy's set at the DMC 1998 USA Final, DJ Scratch's legendary routine with Big Daddy Kane, and Four Color Zack's work at The Do-Over all showcase different takes on this technique. I noticed that no one in the breaking scene was doing it, so I decided to incorporate it into my mixes.

The final section of the mix took a more b-boy approach, featuring undiscovered breakbeats and the emerging wave of production-based breaks that only a handful of people were making at the time. It was a perfect opportunity to preview Paten Locke and my unreleased track "The Good Foot". After playing it at the Red Bull BC One World Final in 2013, people had been asking about it, so this mix gave them a teaser.

While this mix was one of my most thought-out projects, it only took me a day to finish the 49-minute set, with just one revision. I guess I was lucky with this one!

• Mix cover by Kenski (2015).

Free In The Style Vol. 2 - January 10, 2015

Free In The Style Vol. 1 is my most popular mix, but Vol. 2 had a much bigger impact on today's breaking music culture. In my opinion, the music from Vol. 2 helped define the sound of the Red Bull BC One. Most of the tracks from this mix are now classics in the Red Bull audio library. It was also the first time I made a mix using songs I created and curated specifically for Red Bull BC One.

At the time, there weren't many mixes with original breaking music material in heavy rotation, so making this mix was a unique experience. It was the first time I worked directly with some of the best producers and musicians globally, including B. Bravo, Falcons, Mr. Carmack, Teeko, Fusik, J-Zone, Two Fresh, Promnite, and Cha Cha Malone. I had only 31 songs to work with, and I intentionally didn't use any records I dug up for the first time in my career. I knew I had to stick to this because of the momentum I had after DJing back-to-back at the Red Bull BC One.

The breaking scene was eager for the tracks I played at the Red Bull BC One World Final in 2014, so I had a strong starting point. Many of the songs were already paired from battle sets I played during that event, which made it easier, but the real challenge was the transitions between songs that weren't pre-paired. This mix turned into more of a production-based project rather than just a blend of tracks. There were moments where I had to break down the records, using specific parts of songs to make smooth transitions.

For example, transitioning from Starship Connection's "Suns of the Pharaoh" to "Desert Sands" was tough because they didn't naturally blend. I ended up editing both tracks, creating a clean drum loop from "Suns of the Pharaoh" and transitioning it into the break of "Desert Sands." This allowed me to layer them seamlessly, despite their heavy instrumentation. It took a few days of trial and error to get the flow right.

Making a mix is like putting together a puzzle – sometimes you have to search for the right pieces to fit. This mix took two weeks to finish, with around five revisions for the 27-minute section. I wrapped it up a month after DJing the Red Bull BC One World Final in 2014 and spent a lot of time making sure the song transitions were as close to perfect as possible, with special attention to key matching.

Hearing the flawless transitions from DJs in LA at that time pushed me to raise my mixing game. The result is a high-energy mix, specifically designed for breaking competitions. While it may not have been my favorite in terms of pure musical artistry, its impact on the sound of breaking events today is undeniable, especially with the rise of production-based tracks. Shout out to B Ryan for adding his section of the mix after mine!

• Mix cover by Spen One (2019).

Live @ Styles No Jokin - August 3, 2019

Live @ Styles No Jokin is one of my favorite mixes, mainly because it was the first time I incorporated every era of Hip Hop into one continuous journey. At 80 minutes, it's the longest mix I've ever made, and it takes listeners through different periods of Hip Hop music. From the classic 1970s NYC park jam vibe to today's present-day sound, this mix is a true reflection of the genre's evolution.

What makes it unique is that portions of the mix were recorded live during the event, which made it tricky to put together. Essentially, it's four different mixes combined into one. While I made minor edits to smooth some transitions, the core of the mix remains live.

I started by playing newer Hip Hop, gradually moving into the late 1990s and early 2000s. Then, I dropped some new funk, 1980s rap, classic 1980s electro (dedicated to Float, RIP), 1970s breakbeat anthems, rare 1980s breaks, and finished with an Afro Funk vibe.

These days, it's rare to hear such a variety of eras in a mix. For me, this was about paying homage to the legends and educating the younger generation of Hip Hop heads. My experience playing with pioneers at park jams in NYC really helped me channel that spirit. I gave it my own flavor, though, and after hours of edits and listening on no sleep, I managed to complete it in just 36 hours.

• Mix cover by Kenski (2021).

Now Serving! - May 17, 2021

I made this mix to bring back an old breakbeat sound with some newer Hip Hop tracks that barely ever get played at breaking events. I added a few produced beats to satisfy some of the younger breakers, but I tried to refrain from overdoing it. There is an extreme focus on production-based breaks in the breaking community in the 2020s, which makes everything feel a little off-balance.

It's essential to provide a variety of music to keep the dance exciting because that's what keeps the vibe fresh. This is how Hip Hop culture has always been progressive. Throughout breaking history, DJs have continually played from different genres, eras, and music with different feels rather than sticking to one specific style. When production-based breaks become too formulaic and predictable, breakers tend to force their movements to hit a freeze on the one, rather than being more spontaneous with their movements and flowing with the music.

I didn't make a full breaking mix for almost two years, and I also took a break from DJing for a few months. Initially, this mix was in the works in April 2021, but I didn't feel my music selection was up to par with my standards. I was frustrated with it and knew I couldn't put it out. I felt a little rusty with my DJ skills and wasn't back in the DJ zone yet due to the pandemic layoff.

I spent an extra month going the extra mile to dig for more tracks and practice my DJ skills. I knew Now Serving! had to be a statement mix to bring back some balance. It was challenging to complete because I had two different sections that didn't initially fit together. One section was Hip Hop tracks that were 95–103 BPM, the next featured some of my produced beats and new funk songs in the 110–115 BPM range, and the final section was classic and rare breaks, with a BPM range of 115–125.

I drew inspiration from the J Dilla and Madlib sound in the first section of the mix: the gritty samples, the swung-out drums, and the legendary sample chops. I've always loved dancing to their music, but sadly, their tracks get overlooked at most breaking events. I used some of their beats, along with others by producers they've inspired.

House Shoes was another influence for the first section, after having him play at a few of my events. I love how he never makes safe choices in the music he plays. He spins a lot of dope Hip Hop instrumentals and under-the-radar rap joints. Thanks to Shoe's blessings, I included 14KT's "Understanding" remix instrumental from his Street Corner Music label, which helped glue the first Hip Hop section together.

A little further into the Hip Hop section, I found King Micah's "Indigenous Gems" the day before I started recording. It made the transition from the Hip Hop section to the produced beat section much smoother. After King Micah's first verse, you hear a Kung Fu vocal sample with no drums, so it was easy to bring in the intro of my track "Fire Starters" over the vocal sample, bumping up the mix by 5 BPM. After a few minutes in the produced beats and new funk section, I returned to the traditional sound we rarely hear in the 2020s. This section came from record digs I had done over the years, including some breakbeat classics.

This part was easier to put together, but I had to cut up different portions of songs to get the right transitions. For instance, it was tricky to get a clean transition from Carl Sherlock Holmes' "Investigation" to the rare German break I used afterward. I had to manually loop different portions of the Carl Sherlock Holmes track to get the right flow for the transition. I skipped from 1:27 to 1:55, right when the horns would end, and brought the German break in just before the second break of "Investigation" started. Thankfully, my production skills helped me quickly figure out how to make it work.

As far as original selection and a pure breakbeat approach, this is one of my favorite mixes I've made. It shows my maturity as a DJ, who just wanted to create a mix with music I enjoy listening to and offer something I felt the scene needed. The process of creating this 30-minute mix took over a month, but it was all worth it.

MY PHILOSOPHY ON DJING AT A BREAKING EVENT

• Always had the best view. Freestyle Session World Final in San Diego, CA (2019).

Photo: Carlo Cruz

In recent years, breaking events have largely catered to one specific crowd: the breakers. As long as you keep your playlist focused on up-tempo boom bap, Hip Hop, and funk, you're generally in a safe zone. However, the most challenging aspect of DJing for breaking is finding the right music, as very little music is explicitly created for the art form. Tracks like "Apache" and "It's Just Begun" are considered breakbeat classics, but they were not originally intended for breaking. They just happen to have the rhythm and soul that get b-boys and b-girls to go off. Digging for the perfect tunes is a slow but essential process.

To prepare for an event, I typically spend several hours researching the city I'm playing in and determining the demographics of the attendees. This helps me gauge how my music taste might align with theirs. Over the years, I've spent almost two decades refining my style through research, mixing, digging, and creating music. I dedicate two full days, about six hours each, to curate new playlists or mini-sets for an event, striving to play music that other DJs don't, or to revive forgotten gems.

Every set I perform is unique because most events I DJ at are streamed or up-loaded to YouTube, and I want to ensure I'm offering something new and exciting. Not every audience has the same taste, and it's crucial to read the room and control the dance floor, much like understanding human psychology by reading the dancers' body language.

The Cipher Approach

One of the first techniques a DJ must master for breaking events is the cipher approach, which is similar to DJing a party. During cipher time, when dancers are just warming up or taking turns, it's an excellent opportunity to showcase your DJ skills. This is your time to control the vibe, to make the crowd feel all kinds of emotions. If you're DJing for a few hours, you need to keep things fresh and interesting.

Classic boom bap Hip Hop and lesser-known funk breaks are perfect for cipher time. If you're DJing at the start of an event, begin with slower tracks (around 90–97 BPM) and gradually build the energy with more up-tempo tracks as the event progresses. Try to keep it under 120 BPM to avoid tiring out the dancers. It's all about pacing, avoiding jumping between BPMs too quickly. I usually play five songs in the same BPM range before adjusting the speed.

If I'm headlining and scheduled to play during peak cipher times, I often opt for a high-energy set. There's a clear difference between playing for an older crowd, who tends to favor the traditional classic Hip Hop sound, and a younger generation of breakers, who generally prefer newer sounds.

For events with mixed dance styles or a more general audience, I expand my playlist to include party tunes, like house music and popular Hip Hop. These sets are usually my favorite to play. A great example is The Notorious IBE festival in the Netherlands, where the balance of different dance styles and the non-breaking Dutch audience creates a great opportunity to play varied music.

The Battle Approach

The second approach is the battle format, where b-boys and b-girls dance directly to the music you provide. In this setting, your job is to keep the energy high and the crowd engaged. Pay attention to the dancers, especially the veterans or those with a high level of musicality, if you see them head-nodding, that's a clear sign you're playing the right music.

During battles, dancers often get frustrated if a DJ overshadows the music with excessive scratching or looping while they're trying to dance. While technical skills are vital, music selection is paramount for catering to dancers. As long as you maintain a smooth flow with your transitions and play the right tracks, dancers will stay engaged and happy.

I aim to keep the music funky, with drum timbres that match tracks like James Brown's "Soul Pride," funk rhythms, and non-quantized grooves. I typically avoid breakbeats above 125 BPM, staying within the 100–125 BPM range for battle music. There are exceptions, like Mongo Santamaria's "Cloud Nine," but generally, I keep the tempo lower.

For battle sets, I select high-energy tracks that maintain the vibe, like Wu-Tang Clan's "Uzi (Pinky Ring)," up-tempo breaks such as the one in Titanic's "Love Is Love," and classic funk like Donald Austin's "Side Saddle." Quick mixing is essential. I start battles with tracks that have a clean intro, but not one that's too long, follow-up tracks should flow seamlessly, without prolonged intros. Ideally, the next track should go straight into the beat or groove of the record.

Matching the energy of the last track is critical, never let the momentum drop. Bring in the next record as soon as a dancer finishes their round or when the next competitor comes out. Most breakers will dance between 30 seconds to a minute, usually finishing with a freeze or spin-up.

Scratching the next track in is a great cue for the dancers, signaling that a new song is coming in. It's essential to pay attention to the dancers' movements and keep track of which track they're responding to. Aim to play a song for no longer than two minutes, giving dancers on both sides of the floor an equal chance to showcase their skills.

Featuring a variety of breakbeat and Hip Hop music, with or without lyrics, is essential for maintaining fresh energy in battles. The breaking community is relatively small, so I often know the music preferences of most dancers, but I take chances when uncertain. I think of playing music in between battles as providing theme music for the dancers, an idea inspired by the Notorious IBE, watching WWE or boxing as a kid.

Between battles, I always recommend keeping the music flowing. Dead air can drain the energy in the room, and the event's momentum can quickly fade. When the music stops, the atmosphere can become awkward, often leading to excessive talking by the host. The vibe is crucial to maintaining a great event, and if you have the freedom, make sure the music keeps playing!

There have been times when my DJ performance fell short and negatively impacted the battle. For instance, at Undisputed 2017 in Prague, I had one of my worst DJ performances. A panic attack a month before the event left me mentally unprepared. I didn't properly prepare my DJ selection, skipped soundcheck, and neglected technical checks, which resulted in technical issues. These small details matter, things that a novice DJ might overlook, but they're critical for delivering a great performance.

To sum it up: DJing at a breaking event requires a deep understanding of both the dancers' needs and the event's atmosphere. To create an unforgettable experience, DJs must master music selection, maintain smooth transitions, and stay prepared. Mistakes happen, but learning from them is what allows us to grow as DJs and elevate the experience for the breaking community.

• Getting inducted into the Berklee Hip Hop Hall of Fame in Boston, MA (2024). Photo: Muriel Florence Rieben

• With Olympic bronze medalist B-boy Victor Montalvo and Sway Calloway on Sway in the Morning in Manhattan, NY (2024).

• With my Red Bull family at the Red Bull BC One World Final in Manhattan, NY (2022).
Photo: Carlo Cruz

• With Victor Montalvo, Paulskeee, Dr. Abby Wolf, Logistx, and El Nino at
Harvard University in Cambridge, MA (2024).

Photo: Evgenia Eliseeva

• Behind the scenes at Red Bull Lords of the Floor in Seattle, WA (2024).

Photo: Little Shao

• Photo: Evgenia Eliseeva

Lino "Lean Rock" Delgado is a world-renowned DJ, international breaking champion, and acclaimed music producer whose deep Hip Hop roots have taken him to over 30 countries. Born into the culture as a member of Boston's legendary Floorlords, he has mastered both breaking and DJing over 25+ years, earning recognition as a thought leader, historian, and mental health advocate. He is officially recognized by both the governor of Massachusetts and mayor of Boston for his groundbreaking contributions—the first U.S. DJ/B-boy to receive such honors.

Paul Vincent Ruma has spent over three decades documenting and shaping Hip Hop culture. As the co-author of this memoir, he worked closely with Lean Rock to capture and preserve his remarkable journey. A proven leader in skill development and education, he has coached and mentored generations of DJs and breaking champions through his M.E.B.T.R.I.L.L. training framework since 1998, most recently guiding 2024 Olympic medalists and breaking world champions from five countries. As the founder of Mighty4 and co-founder of Out For Fame, the USA's first national breaking championship, his seminal events helped elevate breaking into a global competitive art. In 2024, alongside Lean Rock, he made history at Harvard University's Hiphop Archive & Research Institute with *Breaking Boundaries*, the first formal recognition of breaking at an Ivy League institution. Pursuing a PhD in Sociocultural Anthropology at UNLV and co-founder of Scholars of Style, he bridges Hip Hop culture and academia—staying true to his *always a student* ethos while preserving and evolving the culture worldwide.